Alisa Grunert

NBIC Technologies as Weapons of Modern Warfare

WIFIS-aktuell
Book Series

Edited by

WIFIS – Academic Forum for International Security, represented by

Prof. Dr. Johannes Varwick, Martin Luther University Halle-Wittenberg

Volume 83

Alisa Grunert

NBIC Technologies as Weapons of Modern Warfare

Verlag Barbara Budrich
Opladen • Berlin • Toronto 2026

A CIP catalogue record for this book is available from
Die Deutsche Nationalbibliothek (The German National Library):
https://portal.dnb.de.

Carbon compensated production

ISBN 978-3-8474-3442-9 (Paperback)
eISBN 978-3-8474-3386-6 (PDF)
DOI 10.3224/84743442

Verlag Barbara Budrich GmbH
Stauffenbergstr. 7. D-51379 Leverkusen Opladen, Germany | info@budrich.de | www.budrich.eu

86 Delma Drive. Toronto, ON M8W 4P6 Canada | info@budrich.de | www.budrich.eu

Cover design by Walburga Fichtner, Cologne, Germany
Typesetting by Angelika Schulz, Zülpich
Printed in Europe on FSC®-certified paper by paper&tinta, Warsaw

Preface

Against the backdrop of increasingly blurred boundaries between military and civilian technology development, the migration of conflict into the cognitive domain as well as the geopolitical rivalry between the United States and China, this study addresses a field of considerable strategic relevance. It examines a highly topical and security-relevant issue: the convergence of nanotechnology, biotechnology, information technology, and cognitive science (NBIC) in the context of modern warfare.

The central research question is: "How do scholars assess NBIC technological convergence in relation to modern warfare at the beginning of the 21st century?" This overarching question is operationalized through three sub-questions: Where does the convergence of the individual NBIC technologies become relevant? How are the NBIC disciplines interconnected within the logic of dual use? And how can NBIC technologies be classified from an offensive–defensive perspective?

An integrative literature review serves as the methodological framework—an appropriate approach for a field that remains only partially explored. The dataset, comprising nearly 50 publications over a period of 21 years (2004–2025), provides a solid empirical basis. The development of a model to visualize processes of "weaponization" also constitutes a genuine conceptual contribution. The nexus between doctrine/strategy, technological development, technological deployment, and effects/consequences—conceived as a dynamic and recursive relationship—is plausibly elaborated. The cartographic representation of technological convergences offers an original synthetic approach. The study of a double shift—from the classical civil-military dual-use dichotomy towards a useful–harmful understanding, and from the offensive-defensive distinction toward an overt–covert differentiation—emerges a clear analytical finding on which further works can build.

This work was written as a master thesis within the framework of the Research Group on Arms Control and Global Order at the Institute of Political Science at Martin Luther University Halle-Wittenberg. Interdisciplinary research projects conducted there examine state positions on the regulation of disruptive military technologies and critical raw materials in international forums.

Berlin/Halle (Saale), March 2026

Prof. Dr. Johannes Varwick
Chairman of the Academic Forum
for International Security – WIFIS e.V.

Table of Contents

List of Tables and Figures

Abbreviations

4IR	4th Industrial Revolution
5GW	5th Generation Warfare
AI	Artificial Intelligence
BBB	Blood-Brain-Barrier
BCI	Brain-Computer-Interface
BTWC	Biological and Toxins Weapon Convention
BWC	Biological Weapons Convention, also BTWC
CBRN	Chemical, Biological, Radiological, Nuclear
CNS	Central Nervous System
COGINT	Cognitive Intelligence
CRISPR	Clustered Regularly Interspaced Short Palindromic Repeats ("gene scissors")
CS	Conceptual Structuring
CWC	Chemical Weapons Convention
DARPA	Defense Advanced Research Projects Agency
DEW	Directed Energy Weapons
DNA	Deoxyribonucleic Acid (genetic information carrier)
DURC	Dual Use Research of Concern
e.g.	exempli gratia (for example)
EDT	Emerging Disruptive Technologies
EMF	Electromagnetic Fields
EU	European Union
FTR	Facial Recognition Technology
GNR	Genetics, Nanotechnology, Robotics

GZC	Gray Zone Conflict
H/nB	Human/Neuromorphic Brain-Computer-Interface
HW	Hybrid Warfare
ibid.	ibidem (in the same place)
i.e.	id est (that is)
IAEA	International Atomic Energy Agency
IDF	Israel Defence Forces
MAD	Mutually Assured Destruction
MCF	Military-Civil Fusion
MoD	Ministry of Defense
NATO	North Atlantic Treaty Organization
NBCW	Neurobiochemical Weapons
NBIC	Nanotechnology, Biotechnology, Information Technology, Cognitive Science
NPT	Treaty on Non-Proliferation of Nuclear Weapons
PLA	People's Liberation Army
R&D	Research and Development
RAM	Restoring Active Memory
RF	Radio Frequency
RMA	Revolution in Military Affairs
RNA	Ribonucleic Acid
S&T	Science and Technology
tech	Technology
US	United States
WMD	Weapons of Mass Destruction

1 Pertinence of Modern Warfare and New Technologies

Si vis pacem, para bellum.
– *Latin proverb* (Gut 2025)

You have to prepare for war in order to create peace, according to the widely used Latin proverb. Indeed, the past couple of years have indicated this shift towards intensified preparation for war. Over the last decades and especially in recent years, the characteristics of 21st century warfare have shown to be highly accelerating, and new technologies are vital in that sense. Consequently, the antiquated dichotomous understanding of war and peace makes it necessary to look closer into that grey zone which is neither war nor peace (Montocchio 2021: vii). Commonly known hybrid threats can be identified in e.g. cyberattacks or disinformation campaigns and are enabled by progress in information technologies. They evolve from a diverse set of interconnected domains. The interdisciplinary look towards NBIC technologies seems to be particularly relevant in this matter as they comprise ramifications for civilians and the military, which can cause them to be dual use technologies.

NBIC technologies refer to nanotechnology, biotechnology, information technology, and cognitive (neuro-)science. More than 20 years ago, NBIC started to be a scientific project formalized through the Defence Department of the United States in 2002 (Claverie and Cluzel 2022: 9). Bernard Claverie and François du Cluzel describe that:

> "the object is to encourage the development of tools and adapt or improve humans through an anthropo-technical approach to develop a hybridized man system to meet health, security, defence objectives and prepare them for specific bioenvironments (space, sea, deserts, etc.)" (ibid.).

From a civil-military perspective, they contain substantial potential for influence and manipulation, but also enhancement. A race on critical and emerging technology can already be witnessed internationally, the US and China playing major roles based on their efforts to lead the way (Rosenbach et al. 2025: 9). In a study by Rand from 2025, this US-China competition could find a stabilizing factor in improved dialogue and understanding that contain concepts such as a world created by emerging technologies (Mazarr et al. 2025: 84).

New technologies are a hot topic for several actors: The European Union (EU) tries to improve its autonomy in crucial sectors. In a press statement from September 2025, the EU Commission announced to launch a new strategy to strengthen research and technology infrastructures in Europe (European Commission 2025). This was due to the so-called Draghi report, a document on future European competitiveness that emphasizes the EU's weakness in emerging technologies, which are in turn the drivers for future growth (European Commission: European Political Strategy Centre 2025: 5). Similarly, the EU as a whole is currently not at the forefront of defense innovation: International comparison shows notably more spending for such investments in the US, China, Russia, India, but also France (Clapp 2022).

To date, different terminologies exist to classify these new technologies. Still, the terms of emerging, disruptive and converging technologies are often used simultaneously without clear denotation of the scope. Emerging disrupttive technologies (EDT) are known in combination to describe potentially revolutionizing technologies for warfare. Where NATO describes disruptive technologies as innovations with major or even revolutionary effects on NATO defense and security, the European Defence Agency (EDA) identifies them as:

> "quantum-based technologies; artificial intelligence (AI); robotics and autonomous weapons systems; big data analytics; hypersonic weapons systems and space technologies; and new advanced materials" (Clapp 2022).

Some technologies might not be emerging (but repurposed) and lack an emergent or disruptive character per se or are not ready yet to be certainly classified as disruptive. To define NBIC technologies, the most reasonable term of *converging technologies*[1] will be used in this work as the core interest lies in the overlapping of these technologies.

With the rising capabilities of the respective technologies, due to Artificial Intelligence in particular (Shanahan 2015), – non-kinetic weapons find their way into civil life on the one hand and military equipment on the other – creating new security challenges worldwide.

The Second Gulf War demonstrated that advanced technological equipment can cause superiority within a conflict, and simultaneously the Vietnam War has shown that without knowledge on how to deploy equipment correctly, technological superiority does not necessarily have a strong impact (Citino 2012; Steiniger 2020).

1 The definition of technological convergence in a utilitarian sense is the tendency for diverse systems to evolve, blend, and also synergistically reinforce and reciprocally interact which leads to the production of new and unique metatechnological innovations (McCreight 2013: 12).

With the altering of the contemporary global order there comes the necessity of access to emerging features. Why are explicitly converging technologies important in that regard, particularly in recent years? And what links to modern warfare are there to specifically focus on NBIC technologies? The following chapter provides some background to these points and connects it to the research question of this work.

2 Background and Research Question

Dulce bellum inexpertis.
– Desiderius Erasmus of Rotterdam

War is sweet to those who have no experience of it – a quote from Erasmus who positioned himself pacifistically against war in due course. We cannot know for certain what stand he would take today, but we can adopt one of our own – on the condition that we possess the indispensable knowledge on it. As to contribute to this needed body of knowledge, scrutinizing a particular component of the technological process is inevitable: its weaponization. Technological innovations have always and still shape our live – from the Global Positioning System (GPS) to the internet. With these complex changes in everyday life there comes potential for the malevolent under the auspices of modern warfare. Converging technologies within NBIC are of high importance in that matter as the process of weaponization might turn them into weapons. Today, they seem to be subject to changed restrictions – or opportunities. Quite a few years ago, nanotechnology, biotechnology, information technology and cognitive science entered discussions on emerging issues within this field.

What had started as a scientific project in the early 2000s by the US Defence Department underlies different preconditions now, taking into account that Artificial Intelligence (AI) expedites research: What human brains would have needed several years for can now be done with the help of AI in just a few weeks or months (Shanahan 2015: 158). Genetics and neuroscience for instance depend more and more on big data when it comes to scientific discoveries in these fields and AI models are therefore used to identify patterns in a huge amount of data (ibid.: 109).

The potential of these new technologies goes hand in hand with the risk of a new arms race like Murray Shanahan, Professor for Cognitive Robotics in London explains:

> "At first, the chief motivation for developing a powerful weapon is the worry that the other side (whoever they are perceived to be) will get there first. This worry is enough to overcome any initial moral reservations. Then, when both sides have the weapon, an arms race ensues" (Shanahan 2015: 155).

At the same time, security and defense have heavily stepped up again in public debates and policy. With the growing role of non-kinetic warfare, there comes the dual use aspect into play. The initial understanding comes from the synergy between civilian and military areas. For dual use technologies, the civil sector is of high relevance, containing substantial benefits for the military sector and vice versa. In certain cases, dual use in a newer sense might also refer to the same technologies being used in a legitimate way for human betterment and simultaneously misused for malicious reasons, thus for both useful and harmful purposes (Kosal and Huang 2015: 94f.). In this work, dual use is defined as civilian and military applicability.

A more concrete illustration of civil-military exchange will be investigated shortly at this point. The example of Israel demonstrates the relevance and dynamics that flow back and forth in civilian manufacturing and military adaptation. In the past 25 years, Israeli civil-military technological integration intensified so much that its success can be seen in top-ranks of Israeli arms producers worldwide. Israeli defense industries accumulate 75 to 80% of total income by arms exports (Evron 2025: 301ff.). With the Fourth Industrial Revolution (4IR) – comprising technologies like AI, big data, quantum computing or autonomous systems – the pursuit of emerging technologies grows. In the Israeli case, this military-civil fusion (MCF) in the field of science and technology (S&T) signifies the locating and assimilating of civilian technologies in military tools but also the strategic approach of finding respective technologies and producers in order to harness their abilities for a collaboration and finally adapt advanced civilian tech to the military. Since around 2010, Israel's defense industry started to heavily rely on the civilian high-tech industry, which brought the country at the forefront of international military tech innovations (ibid., 309f.).

This general civil-military cooperation in converging technology serves as a factor to keep in mind when analyzing the NBIC literature as some weaponized technologies already exist in a civilian area or are being researched. Another difficulty comes along in terms of the deployment of applicable technologies. A certain application might be used in reaction to an attack, thus either in an offensive or defensive way towards other people. This model was predominantly used at the end of the 20th century to understand the conditions of conflict and cooperation and potential instability due to technology (Kosal and Putney 2023: 83). Taking it into account in this context is still meaningful to provide an analytical basis for researching potential weapons.

Nanotechnology has become a key element of military research because of its components ranging from 1 to 100 nanometers[2]. This way, nano tech operates at atomic and molecular levels. It comes into play in the context of

2 For comparison: The DNA double helix is around two nanometers in width (Kosal 2009: 6).

identifying CBRN[3] threats or – at the intersection with information technology – when it comes to the development of miniature, high-efficient and high-performance electronic elements. These components allow sophisticated communication networks with greater resistance to interference and are more difficult to detect by opponents (Ortmann 2024).

Biotechnology provides the environment for bioweapons. As Covid-19 has demonstrated, viruses can substantially slow down societies and – regardless of where SARS-CoV-2 origins truly lie – the overall impact lasts longer than the symptoms of the disease (WHO 2026).[4] In a more pointed way, DNA (deoxyribonucleic acid) profiling holds the possibility to design genetic weapons for targeting ethnic groups or minorities. In a thought experiment, French President Emmanuel Macron's DNA could be used to determine which diseases he might have and to exploit knowledge about unknown relatives and ancestry. Artificial DNA molecules can even be created in a laboratory in a long and complicated process to mimic a real person's DNA to falsely implicate them in a crime scene (Swedish Defence University 2025). But non-synthetic ways of bioweaponry exist as well, as was witnessed in the deadly Anthrax Attacks in the United Stated in 2001 (Federal Bureau of Investigation 2016).

Information technology probably serves as a key technology when controlling new innovations in the related science fields. An exemplary intersection of bio- and information technology is remotely controlled cockroaches as bio robots – a project that is pursued by the German Startup Swarm Biotactics to deploy respective cockroach cyborg swarms for defense and rescue missions in the future (Schimroszik 2025). Additionally, cyber attacks on critical infrastructure such as ports in Lisbon, Antwerp or Marseille have become commonly known (Senarak 2024). Those cyber threats, like theft, manipulation or unauthorized access with malicious use, are a real concern.

Cognitive Science intersection with information technology lies by way of example in Brain Computer Interfaces (BCI). Especially neuroscience in this regard is needed to mirror brain structures or enhance the human brain through enlargement of the prefrontal cortex[5] by expanding the neuron count

3 The abbreviation CBRN signifies chemical, biological, radiological, and nuclear threats. In contrast to the previously used term of NBC (nuclear, biological, chemical) dangers, CBRN threats are internationally used to identify such risks today (Bundesamt für Bevölkerungsschutz und Katastrophenhilfe 2025).

4 The Covid-19 Pandemic leaf to the largest disruption of the education system to date. Despite the unknown long-term consequences, evidence shows negative impacts in education, safety, resilience, and connectedness. Particularly mathematics and science report a fall in competences for students from more vulnerable and deprived backgrounds (WHO 2026).

5 The prefrontal cortex is linked to working memory which is substantial for powerful cognition (Shanahan 2015: 94).

(Shanahan 2015: 94). Cognitive Science can probably be anticipated to play a growing role in what the French scholars Claverie and du Cluzel call "Cognitive Warfare" (CW). Here, the circle closes as the intertwining with technologies from nano- and biosciences are essential in determining both potentials and risks of an emerging warfare concept.

The exemplary section above gives a brief overview of relevant scenarios in the convergence of nano-, bio-, information technology and cognitive science. Looking from a modern and future warfare point of view, the progression of such innovations seems meaningful to analyze for further research. In favor of a representative literature review of these issues to locate linking points for researching NBIC convergence, the following research question (RQ) is used for analysis:

How do scholars assess NBIC technological convergence in terms of modern warfare at the beginning of the 21st century?

Further structuring of the aimed research in this work is done by dividing the RQ into sub questions. These three elements will be central for the review and the answer to the RQ:

- Where does convergence of each NBIC technology come into play?
- How are NBIC disciplines intertwined within the dual-use logic of tools?
- How can NBIC technology be classified from an offensive-defensive point of view?

This study aims to identify core themes of current research within NBIC technologies in terms of their dual use implications and to detect potential gaps in contemporary research of NBIC convergence. As innovations in technical fields are ongoing and the implications for security and defense are still emerging, the review provides a critique of existing literature. The synthesis seeks to bring more clarity to also the defensive and offensive character of converging weapons. Therefore, the next chapter introduces the applied methodology.

3 The Integrated Literature Review

"Integrative literature reviews provide review and critique to resolve inconsistencies in the literature and provide fresh, new perspectives on the topic"
– Torraco 2016: 404f.

As quoted above, the aim of an Integrated Literature Review (ILR) is not a simple overview of research on a topic. It serves as a well-established methodology to combine review with critique and proper synthesis. After the methodological introduction, the identification of relevant literature for the dataset and the conceptual structuring as rough guidance follows.

3.1 Introduction to the Method

Based on the presented background and purpose of the topic, an IRL is chosen to fulfil the research objective mentioned in chapter 2. Converging technologies with particular focus on NBIC are treated as a still emerging topic within the dual use discourse in security and defence. Broadly, the steps of an ILR show how 1) literature was identified, 2) analyzed, 3) synthesized, and 4) reported (Torraco 2005: 630).

For a structured review, the checklist on writing an ILR from Torraco (2005) is used. The analysis follows two steps: 1) a critical analysis of the literature and 2) an integration of diverse and potentially conflicting perspectives from the data. Critical analysis works as a prerequisite for literature synthesis. It therefore aims to show how the literature integrates into broad theories and patterns on the one side. To probe what the future of practice in this field would look like on the other side is simultaneously the goal, as generally little attention is given to this beneficial element of ILR (Torraco 2016: 408f.). Core elements of critical analysis entail discussion about how well the literature represents the topic and a deconstruction of the literature with a contextual view on e.g., social context, research findings or applications to practice (Torraco 2005: 361f.; Torraco 2016: 419f.).

Via this ILR the synthesis is expected to contribute to the theory-building of the emerging NBIC convergence by identifying strengths and weaknesses as well as deficiencies and contradictions among the data (Torraco 2016: 407, 412). Due to the complexity of new technologies, the useful and harmful implications under circumstances of modern warfare become ever more discussed in both scientific and public debates about security. The necessity of such a review is linked to a (potentially) purposeful contribution to current discussions on converging technologies in a security context. Civil-military implications in terms of NBIC tech in modern warfare would benefit from an integrated synthesis of reviewed literature because they can contribute to a preliminary conceptualization of a still emerging topic (ibid.: 409f.). Additionally, theoretical contributions should be important in a way that they are applicable to more than a limited and restricted specific context. Literature synthesis should result in new perspectives and catalyze further research (ibid.: 411, 416).

The structure of the ILR is shaped along practices, programs and interventions in the literature as opposed to other forms in which research methods and theories in the literature are reviewed (ibid.: 405).

With the objectives and definitions above in mind, this approach focuses on reviewing, critiquing and synthesizing literature. As Torraco emphasizes, literature reviews cannot follow a predetermined format to organize the review. Conceptual Structuring (CS) as one part of the review is essential for coherence and clarity and helps to essentialize the main concepts of the topic to come together as a unified idea. For this analysis, the CS consists of a combination of respective warfare approaches (ibid.: 412ff.).

3.2 Identification of Literature

Following the steps of an ILR according to Torraco (2005: 360), relevant literature was first identified through the scientific database JSTOR, but also through respective research institutions such as the Stockholm International Peace Research Institute. JSTOR covers a solid amount of research documents. Additional literature was searched for by using the well-known snowball method or was gathered through recommendations.

Here, the coverage was conducted to a representative degree. The review follows a mostly conceptual setup and targets academics (Torraco 2016: 205). Representative literature is located by searching for certain keywords in different combinations and mostly for each of the four disciplines separately (ibid.). Used keywords include *NBIC Nanotechnology, Biotechnology dual use, NBIC information dual use, information technology dual use modern warfare, NBIC Cognitive Science, cognitive neuroscience weapon, NBIC dual use* and were further combined where valuable for literature research.

This step was combined with a following check to see if literature needed to be excluded or included based on ex ante determined criteria. Second, the analysis is two-staged: abstract reading and skimming are followed by detailed review, complemented with explicit keyword search within texts (e.g. in books) (Torraco 2016: 406; 2005: 361). Literature for this review is *included* if the following criteria are met:

- scientific publications (no lay publications) with a focus on one or more NBIC technologies
- a link to civil-military consequences, such as dual use discussions or security implications
- publications that were published from the early 2000s on as NBIC just appeared around that time, until November 2025
- empirical, theoretical, descriptive publications (scientific articles, reports, book chapters) accepted
- publications were *excluded* if: they present agricultural studies or deal with world food and hunger, economics-, health-, and medicine-related topics only; they were not published in English

The final data set consists of 47 publications covering the past 21 years (2004-2025). Parts of the selected documents are not empirical studies; however, they were chosen as they contribute theoretically to the object of research. Since the topic is treated as emerging, too strict limitations might prevent relevant examinations from appearing and therefore a rather lax narrowing of the body of literature was applied. Also, due to the remarkableness of NBIC convergence in security and defense, recent literature appears more relevant, which is visible in the selected data. Additionally, some papers or book chapters deal with NBIC technology, but partly neither from a security point of view nor with enough depth to critically examine the research topic. Some of these papers are still included as they are relevant for the analysis in general terms and give insight into technological functionality.

For the benefit of structure, a table for the selected studies with their approaches and key concepts was created (Oermann and Hays 2016: 76f.) and will be presented in chapter 4.

3.3 Conceptual Structuring

Knowing that hybrid threats are substantially dependent on technologies (i.e. information technology for cyberattacks) and this field has become distinctly complex, a conceptual structure to guide the review on this topic is essential for its research (Torraco 2005: 359).

For the past decades, defense technology is subject to a broad range of changes that, as a result, lead to new armament dynamics which is being discussed in relation to the Revolution in Military Affairs (RMA) (Prust 2025: 33, Bredow 2024: 93). The RMA – along with the assumption that new types of warfare occur due to military technological transformations and associated doctrinal adaptations – contains the study of technological impact on security policy. Especially network-centric warfare plays a notable role because links between combatants and military platforms have appeared as a result of these technologies as they e.g., facilitate information sharing (Kosal and Huang 2015: 94).

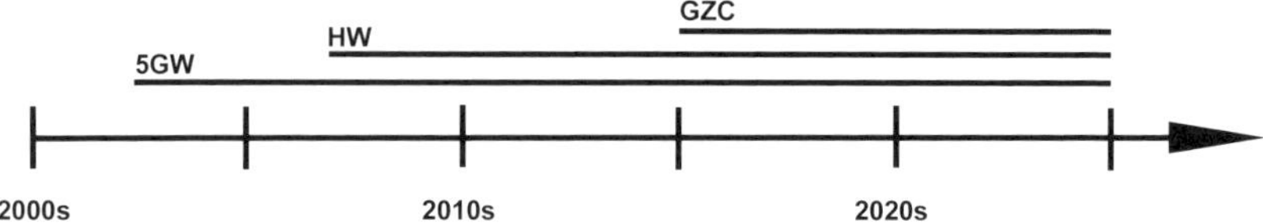

Figure 1: Timeline of warfare concepts, own depiction based on Krishnan 2022.

Such changes shape the military and civilian landscape as the RMA works as an enabler of new warfare imageries. In relation to hybrid threats and hybrid warfare (HW), discussions have evolved around two other terms: fifth generation warfare (5GW) and gray zone conflict (GZC). Even if the ideas behind these concepts are not new, these three schools can be taken to link some of their parts together in order to gain an understanding of war that is adapted to the current issue.

5GW was argued to make former types of military force obsolete as inter alia biotechnology and nanotechnology are viewed as drivers of 5GW. Technological capabilities can be carried out via non-state actors and quite independently from the number of individuals involved, which for instance could lead to destructive bioterrorism attacks by only one person towards a nation state. Another suggestion around the 2010s was to recognize the sprawl of domains in the Information Age that would comprise information, cognitive and social domains in addition to the traditional physical ones of air, land, and sea. The main factor of power would lie in manipulation and deception without the adversary realizing to have acted on behalf of the enemy's will – or without even recognizing that there was a conflict or war at all (Krishnan 2022: 16ff.). This conceptual understanding of 5GW – which is distinctly more popular in South Asia than in Western countries – interleaves with what NATO describes in its 2021 introduced concept of cognitive warfare (Claverie and Cluzel 2022; NATO Review 2021, May 20). Aiming to disrupt societies through built-up mistrust, the human mind is the bull's eye of battles (Krishnan 2022: 18f.).

Secondly, hybrid warfare, with its initial influence from Frank Hoffman, equally builds on the assumption that irregular conflicts would be dominating contemporary warfare. In contradiction to 5GW, HW acknowledges the ability of regular military forces to be relevant in modern conflicts as the modes of war become blurry – in terms of whoever fights or whatever technology is implemented –, leading to complexity that the HW concept addresses. In conventional and unconventional warfare, leveraging technology would occur unpredictable. In this way, HW can be understood as a blend of a state conflict's lethality and irregular warfare. In the context of NATO, HW is primarily used as an umbrella term with special highlight to propaganda and destabilization, encompassing military and non-military elements (Krishnan 2022: 20f.).

GZC as a third school of considered war theories finds its fundament in the realization of a return of a great power conflict. In that sense, GZC tries to address the void of 5GW and HW by assuming that future conflicts take place in a gray area, so ambiguous to blur the line between what is fully war and fully peace. Michael Mazarr from the US Army War College stated in 2015 that revisionist powers would deliberately pursue tactics short of war in order to avoid a full-scale war while still being persistent. Referring to Mazarr, GZC can be identified in four characteristics: (1) Political objectives are pursued via integrated and cohesive campaigns by belligerents, (2) They use non-military and non-kinetic tools, (3) Belligerents avoid escalation on purpose, (4) They count on gradualism. In GZC, various tools and elements of power come together with the aim of circumventing a direct military conflict on a large-scale. As a result, the line between military and non-military actions blurs as well (Krishnan 2022: 21ff.).

GZC gives special attention to the tools that are used by belligerents and does not focus on a specific domain. Conflict therefore can occur anywhere, ranging from peoples to individuals. While GZC is rather linked to a state-actor focus, 5GW and HW emphasize the relevance of non-state actors more. Apart from that, in GZC the importance of civilian instruments is pointed out as they may serve military objectives – which marks the strong connection of military and civilians as combatants (Krishnan 2022: 25).

Both HW and GZC assume that the pursued objectives have an ultimately political nature. GZC, in particular, is pushed forward because of revisionist dynamics, aiming to rise as a state in a US-driven world order but without the high costs of large-scale attacks. For this reason, GZC points out long-term campaigns to disengage adversaries. 5GW on the contrary, stands for undermining the state itself. While 5GW works more efficiently when kinetic force is absent, HW highlights force as a key factor for success, and GZC intends to minimize the use of force to operate below overt aggression (Krishnan 2022: 24ff.).

This hazy line between combatants and civilian population can equally be noticed between regular and irregular warfare – and consequently legal and illegal. Everlasting war becomes a lucrative business for private stakeholders. With a vanishing state as the main actor, regular troops disappear because their legitimacy is linked to a state's monopoly of physical violence. The scope gets broader as more and more tools are applicable as weapons, while this hybridity still operates below the threshold of a military war. To reduce a populations' resilience is the overall goal, which is much easier if highly digitalized countries are targeted compared to less complex and modernized nations (Bredow 2024: 96f.).

From this short overview, topic-fitting parts are extracted to utilize an analytical matrix for the literature review, combining elements from 5GW, HW and GZC to a working definition of modern warfare in this analysis. For a better understanding, they are carried together in the following, giving a brief overview of context and structure for the analytical orientation later on.

Table 1: Analytical Matrix with selected warfare characteristics based on Krishnan (2022).

	Characteristics	**War concept**
Geography of conflict	Multiple domains with special emphasis on tools	GZC
Initiator of action	States, non-state actors	5GW, HW, GZC
Targeted group	Military staff, civilians	GZC
Objectives of action	Political motives	HW, GZC
Role of force	Relevant, but to be reduced where possible	5GW, GZC

This matrix shows the dominance of Gray Zone Conflict for the conceptual guiding of the literature review. Nevertheless, analytical gaps are compensated by adding elements from Hybrid Warfare and Fifth Generation Warfare to make them fit the NBIC disciplines. Those disciplines involved are examined in the civilian and military sphere, implicating that not only states can and should be of analytical interest. Private actors such as tech companies must be considered, too. Modern warfare techniques of non-kinetic character grow in their relevance to harm adversaries, which is why little force is chiefly paid regard to. Since this is intended to be an analysis from a political science perspective, motives in focus ought to be of political nature. Because political objectives are still malleable in their sense, they are operationalized as aspirations to either gain or secure a position of power.

The further review of the literature will consequently be conducted via these constituted sections that emerged from the analytical matrix: 1) Multi domain geography of conflict with emphasis on tools, 2) States and non-state actors as initiators of action, 3) Military staff and civilians as targeted groups, 4) Political motives as objectives of action, 5) Relevant but reduced role of force.

As stated earlier, civil-military cooperation has a high potential for NBIC tools because of their boosting interdependences. The civil-military range of applications becomes less and less separable from each other, which as a result affects the perception of danger in modern societies (Bredow 2024: 85).

Given that the landscape of warfighting under new technological circumstances has changed and persists with volatility, the question on whether defensive or offensive tools matter more in military operations has reemerged (Mayer 2023). In light of the GZC with an increased role of civilians as potential combatants, the defense-offense approach is pursued in this analysis. In general terms, weapons are considered as:

> "tools, devices or substances which, due to their nature and the way they are used as a means of attack or defense in a specific case, are capable of causing damage, incapacitation or serious injury or even death to people" (Meier et al. 2021: 632).

Defensive weapons describe tools that aim to protect the attacked. Thus, its sense is reaction-based. Offensive tools on the other side mean proactively gaining territory or even destroying and weakening the enemy.

All in all, acknowledging these developments and assessments, instead of only thinking about the military side of the above stated revolution, the term *revolution in civil-military affairs* is more appropriate here (Bredow 2024: 96f.).

4 Convergence of Nano, Bio, Info, Cogno in Modern Warfare

"If the Cognitive Scientists can think it
the Nano people can build it
the Bio people can implement it, and
the IT people can monitor and control it"
- Roco and Bainbridge 2002: 13.

This quote from Mihail C. Roco and William Sims Bainbridge expressed the intertwining of NBIC disciplines. Analogous, this chapter will analyze the potential impact of a NBIC convergence on modern warfare, based on selected literature.

4.1 Critical Analysis of Assessments in Literature

For the critical analysis of scholarly work, the next table shows the selected data set literature with the according thematic approach in a timely order, starting in 2004 and ending in 2025 for a first overview.

Table 2: Concept matrix of selected literature.

N°	literature	field	Approach
1	Nordmann 2004	economics, ethics, law	Integration of NBIC as converging tech for economic competitiveness with emphasis on interdisciplinary research but strict separation of civilian innovations from military purposes and applications
2	Carafano 2005	biotechnology. economics, security studies	War in the 21st century as characterrized by rapid advancements in technology, combat services and demography
3	Bosch/ Ham 2007	bioscience, chemical science, law	UNSCR 1540 as international framework to prevent misuse and keep control of potential use of WMD

N°	literature	field	Approach
4	Caduff 2008	biotechnology, social science, public health, ethics	Bio-related research linked to biosafety and biosecurity as it is growing political territory
5	Kosal 2009	technology, national security community social sciences	Revolutionary nanotechnological convergence and nano-enabled technology for chemical and biological defense and counter measures in current development and for possible future threat scenarios
6	Frinking et al. 2009	bioscience, chemical science, nuclear science, public health	CBRN centered case studies on national capabilities in dealing with threats on different levels, including preparedness and awareness also due to dual use aspects
7	Balakrishnan 2011	Information technology, biotechnology, nanotechnology	Fields of application for converging technologies in the case of India's foreign affairs
8	Koblentz 2012	public health, biotechnology, law	Explanatory approach to management of dual-use risks of biotechnology through voluntary guidelines within the US National Strategy for Countering Biological Threats
9	Tennison/ Moreno 2012	neuroscience, ethics, law	Systematic analysis of neuroscience implementation in US national defense environment with focus on ethics
10	McCreight 2013	neuroscience, nanoscience, technology, bioscience, informatics	Interplay of converging technology including AI and information/communication technology for future strategic security
11	Goodman/ Khanna 2013	geotechnology, biotechnology, information technology	US-focused analysis of biotech-geotech-link in dual use context and acceleration of technology innovation and potential disruptions
12	Kosal/ Huang 2015	cognitive science, neuroscience	Scientists' and neuroscientists' understanding and view of security risks and potential consequences of such research and its implications for international security and governance
13	Hayes/ Cavazos 2015	nuclear science, nanotechnology, biotechnology, information technology	Focus on globalized technological acceleration as eliminating necessity for state-based nuclear deterrence strategies

N°	literature	field	Approach
14	Halper 2015	information science, security studies, nano-technology	Application of multi-domain centered technological innovation in the case of Israel
15	Lentzos 2016	biotechnology, security studies, neuroscience, law	Bioweapons potential of pathogens, synthetic biology and neurobiology as recent scientific trends with misuse risk
16	Rychnovská 2016	security studies, ethics, law	Dual use dilemma in life sciences as converged with ethical issues in science governance
17	Krishnan 2016	neuroscience, cognitive science, biotechnology, information technology	Brains as targets of neurowarfare and implementation of biotechnology & neuroscience research in risk assess-ment of future threats
18	Ienca et al. 2018	neuroscience, biotechnology, security studies, ethics	discusses how the neuroscience com-munity should respond to these dilem-mas and delineates a neuroscience-specific biosecurity framework
19	Bruner/Lentzos 2018	law, psychology, pharmacology, chemical science, bioscience, neuro-science	Using psychiatric drugs, brain stimu-lation, brain imaging or neurobio-chemical weapons leads to states leveraging neuroscientific advances for influence, control, and manipulation of human behavior and cognition
20	Kennedy/ Lim 2018	information tech-nology, econo-mics, law	Innovation run in China and US, em-phasizing economic competition and intellectual property theft
21	Nixdorff et al. 2018	nanotechnology, neurotechnology, security studies	Implications assessment of dual use concerns in brain-targeting nano- and neurotechnology
22	DeFranco et al. 2019	neuroscience, bio-technology, infor-mation technology, security studies	Warfare and intelligence implications of neuroweapons and biotechnological innovations with new emerging arenas like cyberbiosecurity
23	DiEuliis 2019	biotechnology, bio-science, infor-mation science, economics	Emerging threats of biotechnology and genetic innovations assessment for the US and emphasis on cyberbio-security with integration of industrial base
24	MacKellar 2019	security studies, nanotechnology, biotechnology, neuroscience	Neuronal interfaces systematization in relation to dual use and offensive/ defensive application in China and US

N°	literature	field	Approach
25	Kania 2019	cognitive science, security studies, biotechnology	Systematic focus on intersection between biotech and cognitive science in Chinese revolution in military affairs
26	Concini/ Toth 2019	space science, nanotechnology	Implementation of dual use nano-technology in space sector
27	Raska 2019	Security studies, information tech-nology, cognitive science	Emerging military technologies as strategic factors in great power rivalry with focus on China, US, Russia
28	Altmann 2020	technology, social science, natural science	Preventive arms control needed due to wider availability, easier access, small-ler systems; shorter times for attack, warning and decisions; and conven-tional-nuclear entanglement of new military technologies
29	Kosal 2020	biotechnology, se-curity studies, ethics	Biological dual use threat perception in reference to internationally located origins of threats to the US
30	Cunningham/ Geis 2020	security studies, biotechnology, law	US-centered approach on strengthe-ned security regulations to control synthetic biology
31	Frieß et al. 2020	biotechnology, se-curity studies, law	US-centered examination of regulatory preparedness for genetically modified organisms with hostile use potential
32	Sharp 2020	information techno-logy, biotechnology, neuroscience, ethics, law	Cognitive enhancement through neuroapplications and potential trans-formation of warfighters to weapons
33	Biberman 2021	biotechnology, security studies, law	US-centered approach on weaponni-zable biotechnology in international relations coupled with disciplines like cyber for genetic warfare
34	Baker 2021	law, biotechnology, chemical science, information tech-nology	Present and future challenges posed by novel weapons in biotechnology and chemical science, emphasizing implications for political and industrial actors in AI era
35	Kania 2021	security studies, biotechnology, in-formation techno-logy	Chinac-centered analysis of innova-tions in converging technologies as drivers for global superiority

N°	literature	field	Approach
36	Hill 2022	neuroscience, security studies, information science	Military significance of novel technologies in neuroscience for deception and enhancement
37	Crowley/ Dando 2023	biotechnology, chemical science, security studies	International bioweaponization and regulation focus with emphasis on dual use and offensive/defensive implications of research
38	Eads et al. 2023	Psychology, security studies, neuroscience	Analysis of neurostrike implications as a modern warfare strategy in China and US
39	Kosal/ Putney 2023	neuroscience, cognitive science, security studies	Cognitive integrity as the core risk in modern warfare and connection to dissemination of neurotechnology in commercial and military sector in China and US
40	McCreight 2024	biotechnology, neuroscience, nanoscience, ethics, information technology	US-centered enhancement possibilities and hostile use risks in era of minds as new battlefields with strong emphasis of technology-integrated scenarios
41	Bromley/ Maletta 2025	law, security studies, informatics, ethics	Militarization of technologies as driver of civil-military blurriness in the case of facial recognition technologies and their export controls
42	Conde/ Whiskeyman 2025	security studies, cognitive science, information technology	COGINT as a new intelligence collection discipline to close the 5GW gap and enable cognitive domain supremacy
43	Gielas 2025	neurotechnology, information technology, security studies	Risk assessment of BCI and NIBS in military decision-making in terms of human enhancement approaches
44	Hensing/ Schlecht 2025	security studies, neurotechnology, cognitive science	Systematic Europe- and Germany-centered approach on weaponized neurotechnology in defense with emphasis on diversity of currently used and researched applications
45	Mantellassi/ Madziwa 2025	neurotechnology, security studies, biotechnology, information technology	Neurotechnology in defense-centered analysis with focus on dual use character, combined with biotechnological innovations

N°	literature	field	Approach
46	Marjanović/ Smiljanić 2025	neuroscience, information technology, security studies, cognitive science	Systematic approach on cognitive warfare and related risks in combination with other advanced technologies for humans, politics, and society as a whole
47	Minvielle et al. 2025	information technology, nanotechnology, security studies	AI, cyber systems, and surveillance systems as the main factors for superiority in future conflicts

Scholars dealt with the respective subtopics of NBIC convergence and its weaponization over the past 21 years (2004-2025). The following assessment types emerged from the literature: strategic / political, financial / Research & Development, ethical, legal, psychological, awareness-related, scenario-related, and theoretical.

4.1.1 Strategic / political assessment

In the early 2000s, the European Union dealt with *converging technologies* in an accordingly named report from 2004 and highlights transformative technologies as major challenges for policy makers. Economic competitiveness and the needs of citizens are addressed primarily, complemented by an agenda setting context for the inclusion of the public and policy concerns (Nordmann 2004: 6f., 19). Here, a strong emphasis on the strict line between military ambitions and the development of converging tech in Europe is drawn. The aim is to avoid destabilizing the international system as the EU's security strategy is committed to the rule-based international order. It also supports disarmament treaties such as the Biological Weapons Convention (BWC) (ibid.: 34).

Strategies on how to deal with potential disruption should involve geopolitical and geoeconomic as well as geotechnical knowledge in the current century. Goodman and Khanna note a critical need for identifying dual use tech. Particularly here are the export loopholes and the necessity to sanction those who violate existing restrictions. With the emergence of exponential technologies[6], the authors adopt the same view as McCreight (2013) and to some extent Balakrishnan (2013) with the expected upend of established

6 With reference to the exponential emergence of technologies, the authors take reference to Moore's law; a rather axiom-like principle named after Intel Corporation Cofounder Gordon Moore. According to it, computing power (number of transistors per square inch on an integrated circuit) would double every two years (Goodman and Khanna 2013: 65).

regimes and a shift of the global balance of power. The potential of such technological innovations in international relations would be underestimated regularly. Goodman and Khanna argue that a policy to support one's own sovereignty first might be insufficient regarding the assumption that states have more control over these issues than it is realistically the case (Goodman and Khanna 2013: 71ff.).

Great nuclear powers are increasingly shifting towards extending deterrence without relying on nuclear weapons anymore and instead rely on conventional forces with more stealthiness and smartness. They are similarly harder to target (Hayes and Cavazos 2015: 263). Globalization and massive urbanization are expected to make traditional state-based nuclear deterrence strategies obsolete, as the targeting of populations becomes increasingly viewed as an absurd strategy (ibid.: 317). Still, the centrality of new weapons (in terms of extended deterrence) remains relevant as highlighted in other scholarly work (e.g. by Tennison and Moreno 2012).

The global landscape is at current defined by a shift from subsidiary to highly integrated processes and dynamics, whereas military sectors actively incorporate technologies developed in the civilian sector, including AI or cloud computing (Bromley and Maletta 2025: 3f.).

In terms of the previously mentioned CBRN threats, the military crisis management shifted to the civilian domain after the terrorist attacks on 11th September 2001, marking a transition of progressive blur between internal and external threats. Frinking et al. emphasize a call for further integration of these two spheres and approaches of civilian crisis management and sustained military operations abroad with the aim to better deal with the general convergence and allocate capabilities efficiently (Frinking et al. 2009: 68, 79).

The fusion and mutual transformation of technologies into dual use meta-technology has the capacity to disrupt the global balance of power and redefine asymmetric warfare, like Robert McCreight stresses (McCreight 2013: 11f.). There is a critical imperative for nations to treat converging technologies as a top strategic priority for the 21st century – to prevent the erosion of global security (ibid.: 19). International actors such as the EU and Russia but also China might pursue independent developmental paths, seeking to establish a separate foundation for control and evolution of such convergences, instead of following the US regime (ibid.: 11-15).

Furthermore, the pursuit of growing global power positions and shifts in the balance of power are increasingly tied to the acquisition of these capabilities in neuroscience and technology, with nations like China establishing vast genetic databases to create a broader knowledge base for potential strategic use (DeFranco et al. 2019: 54-58).

The acquisition of dual use technologies can degrade the dominant state's relative warfighting capabilities in a context of great power interaction (Kennedy and Lim 2018: 554-558). Technological transactions could be curtailed as to protect the position and the preferred international order of the dominant state (ibid.).

Relevant concerns arise from the dual use character of these technologies, which creates a tension between promoting health and providing resources that could be deployed in military operations. Additionally, the authors highlight the risk of non-state actors and other terrorist groups to target neurotechnology, specifically as they are often overlooked internationally (Ienca et al. 2018). In that regard, as Bruner and Lentzos mention, the shift toward geopolitical turbulence and non-state conflict makes the temptation for behaviorral control more acute (Bruner and Lentzos 2019: 97, 116f.).

Nixdorff, Borisova, Komisarenko and Dando (2018) emphasize dual use concerns where advancements in neuroscience are leveraged for hostile manipulation of the central nervous system (CNS) (Nixdorff et al. 2018: 180f.). The development of non-lethal incapacitating agents for law enforcement is part of a major challenge based on some countries' exploitation of loopholes and ambiguities of the CWC under Article II (ibid.: 193-196).

Many countries possess dual use initiatives or military programs that remain closed to international surveillance and inspection (China is exemplary). Adherence to international standards allows for the potential bypass of existing security frameworks (DeFranco et al. 2019: 54-58).

The ascendency of the private sphere in warfare marks a core development of the 21st century, as Carafano (2005) notes. In return, it effectively destroys the nation state's monopoly of use of violence. As these states are obliged to adopt regulations, this task is not expected to be fulfilled by the private sector which would lead to countries being left behind. Carafano (ibid.: 69ff.) argues that in terms of the political system, liberal free market democracies would perform more effectively in mastering the private military capabilities in contrast to authoritarian states (ibid.: 29ff.). Additionally, in Cuba and India there is evidence of sophisticated research programs in the strategic landscape, which indicates that the US would not hold a monopoly. These developments are accompanied by demographic changes with a slowdown of population growth and a rising age of population. Consequently, manpower is lost (ibid.: 68). War would be viewed as a civil activity that spans over the public and private realms where both areas operate under great maintained autonomy (ibid.: 70f.). Rychnovská (2016) deals with the related dilemmas emerging from technological convergence. Security concerns and life sciences both must cope with the ethical dilemmas of how science is governed, which results in an *ethicalization of security* (ibid.: 310). The dual use character of applications thus is challenging in a way that their circulation must be organized and at the same time, implemented by governments (e.g. to pursue monitoring such as mobility of people). As a result, a restructuring of the relationship between decision-makers, scientists and civil population would occur, potentially affecting the democratic accountability of science and the politicization of expertise on the one hand (ibid.: 314ff.). In undemocratic settings on the other hand, such governance policies may lead to a misuse of power within academia, as Rychnovská notes (ibid.: 323).

In Balakrishnan's (2011) study the case of India was examined: diplomatic efforts have increasingly focused on the growing relevance of technology-based challenges in international relations which is a shift primarily carried out by government initiatives in nuclear power, the space sector, and biotechnology (Balakrishnan 2011: 71ff.). A critical point though is found in the lack of support of developed countries like the US, given that nanotechnology is expected to highly impact the international arena through enabling technological innovations at a small scale that could alter global industrial landscapes. It is highlighted that measures against cybercrime have developed, although a genuinely global effort for a convention is still missing. As well as others before, Balakrishnan notes the weaknesses of the BWC due to lacking formal verification regimes and compliance monitoring. These problems represent a gap in political and technical terms, especially as biotechnology advances fast, too (ibid.: 80-85).

An adequate US strategy should prioritize bio tech as a national interest that fosters innovation and competitiveness through defined codes of conduct in order to be capable of biodefence (DiEuliis 2019: 137).

Another case study was pursued with the Israeli security politics which follows a binary attempt: Israel participates in alliances with e.g., NATO members but still maintains independent capacity to pursue national interests. Monitoring Iranian nuclear facilities via personal space reconnaissance is one example, especially where national technological novelties are implemented. Internal security and conventional warfare thus blended often as strategic independence (Halper 2015: 98f.). Israel further pursues to provide allies with subliminal security relevant information as was seen in the case of campaign targeting ISIS (ibid.: 101).

Military interests drive the development of neural interfaces, specifically for controlling weaponry and robotic systems via brain signals. The Defense Advanced Research Projects Agency (DARPA) funds projects such as "silent talk" to explore brain-to-brain communication for strategic advantages (Mac Kellar 2019: 82f.).

For China's case, the RMA and asymmetric advantage are at the forefront of military strategic catalysators: The traditional concept of ''winning without fighting'' (不战而屈人之兵) is central, which remains highly relevant as technology becomes a primary tool for strategic competition during peacetime. Their strategy shift from informatized warfare to intelligentized (智能化) warfare is essential in shaping the new form of combat (Kania 2019: 83-86). Kania describes that by prioritizing military innovation as a national imperative, the Chinese military aims to disrupt the future global military balance in its favor (ibid.: 92f.). This and the approach of technological leadership is largely politically driven by official science policy and the mandates of the 14th Five-Year Plan. China prioritizes resource mobilization to achieve national priorities and mitigate the risks of global interdependence (ibid.: 28-31). The NeuroStrike[7] is pursued by the Chinese government as part of a broader asymmetric warfare strategy to gain a strategic edge over the US and other Indo-Pacific states such as Taiwan, Japan or India. Cognitive Dominance serves as the overall goal, while it can be achieved without fighting and through the implementation of non-kinetic means – potentially triggering an arms race of non-kinetic military tech (Eads et al. 2023: 6-12).

Both the US and China conduct defense research that often blurs the line between applications for protection and offensive deployment. The CWC specifically permits such applications when their development is conducted for inter alia protective purposes (Crowley and Dando 2023: 12). Crowley and Dando observe that China established a DARPA-like research agency to explore the neural foundation of cognition and less lethal weapons (ibid.: 14ff.).

But not only China or the US pursue the converging tech path; Russia does too. These three nations employ four primary competitive strategies: strategies of denial, cost-imposing strategies, attacking a competitor's strategy, and attacking a competitor's political system, as Raska describes (Raska 2019: 76ff.). The resurgence of great power rivalries, particularly in East Asia, has led to intensifying arms competition for advanced military technologies (ibid.).

Gene editing as a biotech innovation has been explicitly categorized as a threat posed by weapons of mass destruction (WMD), alongside nuclear and chemical programs in countries like Russia, China, and North Korea (Kosal 2020: 601). Additionally, historical concerns remain regarding whether Russia's past interests in mood-altering bioregulators truly terminated (Crowley and Dando 2023: 14ff.).

China views biology as a separate war-fighting domain and thus explores offensive capabilities like ethnically targeted bioweapons. Through the "Made in China 2025" plan and civil-military fusion, the People's Republic

7 NeuroStrike is a term coined by Robert McCreight, including different technologies like application of certain frequencies and their according effects (McCreight 2024: 5)

seeks to dominate biotech to drive national power. On the contrary, American experts often rank biotechnology below AI or quantum technology in terms of military transformation, Cunningham and Geis observe (Cunningham and Geis 2020: 56f.).

Mutual limitation remains difficult because states struggle to view national security as embedded within international security (Altmann 2020: 37ff.). Nevertheless, Baker notes that the implementation of AI arms control may not necessarily require a formal treaty but could instead rely on a consoledation of willing states (Baker 2021: 222f.). Marjanović and Smiljanić advise policymakers to balance defensive strategies with democratic principles to secure the state on the one hand and the societal fabric on the other (Marjanović and Smiljanić 2025: 100).

With special focus on the biological sphere of NBIC, scholars have also dealt with legal questions on biological weapons proliferation. The United Nations established the UNSCR 1540 resolution as to fill a gap of WMD proliferation and accordingly terrorism. But in comparison to the nuclear and chemical counterparts – the NPT/IAEA[8], the Chemical Weapons Convention (CWC) and the Organization for the Prohibition of Chemical Weapons – the BWC lacks effectiveness, also due to weak verification regimes (Bosch and van Ham 2007: 215, 218f.). The authors emphasize that a strengthening of national legal frameworks and international mechanisms for cooperation would show a major step towards robust global governance. Still, as low- and middle-income countries ("developing countries") lack the necessary capabilities for law enforcement and complex export control systems, they have to face strategic hurdles compared to countries with the needed capacities (ibid.: 218-224). The dual use verification problem remains because the difficulty to determine if facilities are producing peaceful materials or deadly weapons persists likewise, which was previously seen in chemical weapons deployment in Syria or Russia (Baker 2021: 220f.).

Nearly twenty years ago, the biotechnology field was also characterized by the threat of eliminated scientific investigations. Biotechnology researchers would need to navigate through a politically charged area. The term of biosecurity comes into play here because scientists would actively try to search special materials with unintended consequences and political implycations. Researchers might even modify their findings politically in order to avoid government interference[9] (Caduff 2008: 259f., 273).

8 The Treaty on the Non-Proliferation of Nuclear Weapons and International Atomic Energy Agency.

9 This was for example the case with the Influenza virus reconstruction in 1918, where political arguments were embedded in technical reports to pre-empt biosecurity contestations (Caduff 2008: 262f.).

Approximately ten years ago, the convergence of biological and chemical disciplines was attested to increasingly blur the boundaries between the BWC and CWC (Lentzos 2016: 49). In the United Kingdom, synthetic biology for instance is identified as a top technology for national security, where the need for transparent military research is expressed to prevent the haziness of defensive and offensive work (ibid.: 58). Lentzos stressed calls to establish an expert-led body within the BWC framework and consequently separate scientific discussions from policy considerations (ibid.: 62). In that regard, Lentzos takes a similar but still different stance in context of political control than Kosal and Huang (2015) who stress further institutionalized oversight as a necessity. Effective institutional responses must also address geopolitical uncertainties and the fact that biological materials are difficult to monitor due to their presence in nature and legitimate dual use applications (Kosal 2020: 611).

Similarly to the UK and synthetic biology, the US views genetic weapons as a significant security concern which results in its path of building alliances and global norms with partners like South Korea and India to manage the according risks (Biberman 2021: 18f., 25f.). Biberman notes that genetic weapons can be used for covert warfare or as a form of high-cost signaling to demonstrate the resolution of a conflict via overt intimidation (ibid.: 21f.).

In reaction to bio threats, DiEuliis (2019) focuses on biodefence in her reviewed article. Current biodefence relies on Cold War-era frameworks that must evolve to support a globalized bioeconomy (DiEuliis 2019: 130f.).

Novel invasive environmental biotechnologies and autonomous spread (e.g. via Gene Drives) across borders complicates international treaties like the BTWC as they define hostility to rely on proving intent – which is difficult when a release of e.g., genetically modified insects is framed as a health activity (Frieß et al. 2020: 32).

Nanotechnology as the first element of NBIC was argued to be absent from primary defense and security policy documents in the US, which would complicate capabilities-based planning for the future (Kosal 2009: 127). Kosal (ibid.), who published the selected literature as the result of a report on nano tech in biological and chemical defense, stresses that emerging tactical threats from both non-state and traditional actors in that context need to be addressed via unconventional ways and through adoption of multidisciplinary strategies (ibid.: 108, 121ff.). That path would involve leaping ahead with taking high risks but also getting a high payoff in return: farsighted concepts to deal with nanotech and nanoscience could maintain an edge over opponents. Apart from that, as a potential proliferation of nano-enabled weapons should not be excluded, a respective strategy to limit such development must be international in scope – combined with improved monitoring and cooperation across the world regions (ibid.: 128ff.).

Another strategic assessment was done by Tennison and Moreno (2012), where both authors emphasize geopolitical dominance through tactical advantages in latest warfighting technology and counter-intelligence. Cognitive science or rather neuroscience is targeted for the benefit of warfighter enhancement. Generally, national security interests in a US perspective would be pursued via the neuro tech channel also for other applications such as deception detection. The integration of neuroscience in the military domain is a reality that must be accompanied by transparent discussions on role and limits, especially for the benefit of responsible use in defense frameworks (Tennison and Moreno 2012: 1ff.).

Neuroscientific breakthroughs carry highly relevant implications in terms of dual use potential for the application in security and intelligence contexts, knowing that converging technologies focus on humans, they have consequences for international relations and the social sphere (Kosal and Huang 2015: 93f.). Neuroscientific innovations pose a disruptive technological risk, resulting in a necessity to institutionally oversee them beyond the current regulatory framework. Kosal and Huang underline a strong imperative to do so, aligning state and scientific interests in either useful or harmful convergence – depending on whether both truly align or not. The latter would lead to persecution of scientists via political control (ibid.: 97f.), which was already critiqued by (Caduff 2008) in the biosecurity context. Ultimately, defense-related programs are inseparably linked to broader policy choices concerning military technology and strategic planning (Kosal and Huang 2015: 95).

Neuroscience is a prerequisite for creating a new battleground for conflict, similar to the emergence of the Internet (Krishnan 2016: 6). Strategic applications include the neocortical warfare, which focuses on controlling an enemy's hostile will rather than using physical violence or kinetic weapons (ibid.: 15f.). This can be applied defensively – to suppress conflicts or adjust the perceptions of hostile societies – or offensively – to manipulate the social and political status quo of other states through destabilization, subversion or even regime change (ibid.: 17). With the growing role of neuroscience, neurodeterrence becomes integral to understand real motivations of an opponent and respectively find the most effective strategies to react (ibid.: 18f.).

Bruner and Lentzos (2019) put their focus on neurotechnology, too: Militarization of behavioral neuroscience is driven by its potential to create weapons of influence that can alter the hearts, minds, and political perceptions of individuals targeted. Consequently, intelligence and military operations could benefit from such knowledge about beliefs and cognitive processes (Bruner and Lentzos 2019: 95, 109f.). Insights into cognitive processes would revolutionize command and control through inter-brain communication or target entire groups to optimize psychological operations (ibid.: 107-110).

With the integration of neuroscience and technology into warfare, intelligence and national security reshapes global security overall (DeFranco et al. 2019: 49ff.). Nevertheless, strategically vital elements for military mobility and survival, such as basic logistical innovations in food and water production, are frequently overlooked in strategic assessments (Minvielle et al 2025: 28).

With the emergence of Brain-Computer-Interfaces, states may rely on Article 51 of the UN Charter to justify preventive self-defense against the construction of human/neuromorphic Brain-Computer Interface (H/nB) collaborations. Their sovereignty depends on the ability to anticipate and act against this asymmetric threat before production is complete, given that neither defensive nor offensive measures would be effective and the current legal paradigm does not prohibit an offensive production, as Sharp describes (Sharp 2020: 317ff., 329f.).

A crucial strategic challenge for governments is the dilemma of protecting citizens from cognitive warfare while simultaneously striving to develop their own neurotechnologies to maintain an advantage of geostrategic deterrence (McCreight 2024: 1f., 8).

Simultaneously, cognitive warfare shifts the focus from kinetic operations to achieving multi-domain supremacy through the narrative upper hand[10] and exploitation of mental biases (Conde and Whiskeyman 2025: 3, 9f.).

Apart from that, neurotech is potentially disruptive, Mantellassi and Madziwa emphasize: The potential impact concerning disarmament and arms control on advanced use of neuro tech in the military sphere needs to be developed more broadly. Also, the growing convergence of neuro tech with other emerging technologies such as bio tech needs to be further analyzed (Mantellassi and Madziwa 2025: 31f.).

In that regard, Hensing and Schlecht describe the need to invest in a dual use foundation and to engage more deeply with NATO for improving defense and deterrence – but with particular focus on the EU and Germany (Hensing and Schlecht 2025: 38f.).

10 The authors mention several primary disciplines to address these challenges from an Intelligence Community point of view: Human Intelligence (HUMINT), Signals Intelligence (SIGINT), Imagery Intelligence (IMINT), Measurement and Signature Intelligence (MASINT), Open Source Intelligence (OSINT), Geospatial Intelligence (GEOINT), and Technical Intelligence (TECHINT) (Conde and Whiskeyman 2025: 3).

4.1.2 Financial/ R&D assessment

Biotechnology research is often dual use and the sector itself is considered to be one of the fastest growing commercial sectors globally, which Carafono already attested in 2005 (Carafano 2005: 68-71). As a result, technologies related to biological and chemical weapons are becoming increasingly accessible (Bosch and van Ham 2007: 218f.).

There has been a considerable shift towards dual use research, entailing that almost any type of scientific study may be subjected to review for potential abuse. Chronic uncertainty is to be expected in the research terrain given that mandates and demands on regulations constantly change (Caduff 2008: 259f., 272). Neuroprojects are wide-ranging – from Restoring Active Memory (RAM) to other dual use neuronal interface systems (MacKellar 2019).

A substantial barrier for the defense community was highlighted by Kosal (2009) with the survival of small high-technology start-ups: They often struggle due to limited federal funding and the high risk that a long-term drug development would come with (Kosal 2009: 80). While many federal nanotechnology initiatives in the US are science-driven, whereas defense-related programs are mission-driven, necessitating a better alignment of research priorities to reduce costs and increase output, especially with regard to bridging gaps for effective interdisciplinarity of programs (ibid.: 125-129).

Koblentz (2012) argues that guidelines for the life sciences community should be provided which are designed to help scientists identify information that could be uniquely helpful to actors with ill intent (Koblentz 2012: 133-136).

In the 21st century, the strategic landscape depends on the ability to detect new sources for military innovation and ultimately integrate them into defense planning. Nearly all great powers currently invest in the development of advanced cyber capabilities – from offensive and defensive to intelligence-driven tools (Raska 2019: 96ff.). Simultaneously, the private sector may allow non-state actors to achieve intellectual dominance in the cyber sphere first, taking into account that this sector would have the necessary resources (Sharp 2020: 223ff., 332).

In a multi-country[11] case study on national CBRN capabilities from 2009, the respective authors express the concern of duplicating efforts and the existence of under-capacity in terms of CBRN threat management. From a resource management perspective, the current division of capabilities between safety and security actors may not be financially or operationally optimal (Frinking et al. 2009: 79).

11 Countries considered in this report were: Canada, France, Germany, Netherlands, UK, US (Frinking et al. 2009).

In India's case, the landscape of scientific research was initially shaped by government-funded initiatives. Yet, the private sector eventually became a primary driver in sectors like information technology (Balakrishnan 2011: 71ff.). Even if support from wealthy states like the US were lacking, there are institutions for technological development that emerged and are, for instance, capable of providing fellowships. Balakrishnan underlines financial investment[12] as priority for emerging technologies (ibid.: 81, 85).

Hayes and Cavazos stress the US' focus of research on the convergence of multiple fields, specifically information technology and computation, nanotechnology, and the nano-biotechnology-convergence. This financial and research commitment is intended to produce new weapon systems capable of neutralizing long-distance threats to both homeland security and to enhance military interventions (Hayes and Cavazos 2015: 264). Cunningham and Geis call for US research priorities that should include advanced materials, living sensors, and anti-pathogens (Cunningham and Geis 2020: 61-71).

Halper observes a strong leading position for the Israeli case concerning research in NBIC areas, but also GNR (genetics, nanotech, robotics) (Halper 2015: 109f.). R&D was capable of accelerating this much with the help of partnerships between de Ministry of Defense (MoD) and major defense companies (e.g. IAI) (ibid.: 99, 102).

China's research in that context involves the collection of 1.2 million foreign conference papers for its institutes in national science and technology, Kennedy and Lim describe, and military strength is based on economic resources (Kennedy and Lim 2018: 554-562). Financially, intellectual property theft in cyberspace represents an essential threat, given that it translates into billions of dollars in lost value. The US has blocked significant high-tech investments to prevent financial-technical knowledge from leaking (ibid.: 568-571). National integration of defense research is a primary focus in China, particularly through institutes like the National University of Defense Technology that concentrates on cutting-edge interdisciplinary (前沿交叉) technologies such as biotechnology and quantum technology (Kania 2019). China's party-state system has shown a high capacity to mobilize high resources for research and development (including biotechnology and new materials), which has allowed the R&D funding gap with the United States to begin closing (Kania 2021: 18, 26ff.).

As the Chinese developments do not remain completely untransparent, there are recommendations for the US and allies to accordingly react by in-

12 As an example, the US invested $4 billion in its National Nanotechnology Initiative while India spent 10 billion Indian rupees for its Nano Mission over a frame of five years (Balakrishnan 2011: 85).

vesting in R&D with the target to pursue fostered collaboration and maintained technological parity (Eads et al. 2023: 2ff., 18).

Despite the reduced presence compared to China and the US, the EU targets funding for defense applications. The European Defense Fund and the EU Defense Innovation Scheme specifically aim to help small and medium-sized companies and startups to access resources for military systems. Future proposals and investments would be characterized by a dual use by design approach to support defense and dual use startups (Bromley and Maletta 2025: 4f.)

While Europe is a leader in neurotechnology research, it frequently fails at commercialization due to risk-aversion and a lack of sustained support throughout the innovation cycle (Hensing and Schlecht 2025: 17). To counter the scarcity of capital and data as core impediments for progress, there are calls to mobilize European public funding for translational research and to invest in making anonymized neural data available for innovation (ibid.: 42f.).

In neuroscience, civilian research has outpaced the military one and therefore marks a shift in historical trends where technologies were usually transferred from the military to the civilian sphere. Despite the often national security nature of research funding for neuroscience, the dual use character of such innovations holds potential of technologies to arise from research which was not funded by the military. It can have national security implications nonetheless (Tennison and Moreno 2012: 1ff.). This also includes the development of drugs and elements which intend to cure mental disorders or enhance cognitive functions. There is a significant focus in academic literature on enhancement technologies because they are developed openly, whereas degradation methods and exotic non-lethal weaponized technology are frequently dismissed as aspirational or fictional, as Krishnan describes (Krishnan 2016: 7-10).

With regard to dual use, Goodman and Khanna similarly underscore that research must focus on the identification of respective technologies and the development of strategies to respond to attacks on a nation's technological core. Under the anticipatory Moore's law, research is altering and steers into the broad arena of actors being touched by sophisticated technology (Goodman and Khanna 2013: 71ff.). Dual use research would often be based on cost-benefit analysis where potential benefits are weighed against costs and the probability of technological misuse. As a consequence, openness and profit are confronted with security and secrecy (Rychnovská 2016: 314ff.).

McCreight observes that the development of converging technology is highly driven by multi-disciplinary expertise or funding, which therefore leads to changing interactions between industry, society, and the scientific community – current research in bioinformatics, DNA diagnostics, and molecular electronics serve as an example here (McCreight 2013: 11-15). A similar observation was made by DeFranco and others, underlining the commercialization and market trends where potential economic profit is leveraged in addition to global power aspirations. A comprehensive surveillance of neuroscience requires to monitor the extent of public and private support, the recruitment of researchers and the overall direction of R&D within both university and private sectors (DeFranco et al. 2019: 58ff.). The gap in the ability to forecast how state-sponsored programs and nonstate actors will harness existing neuro S&T for military applications still remains, as not all are accessible to international surveillance and inspection (ibid.).

In terms of financing efforts, the US supports human performance enhancement mostly via the Department of Defense (DoD) and DARPA. Their priorities include the biorevolution or cognitive computing, but also neuroergonomics and robotics – the interest in converging tech is profound (Kosal and Huang 2015; Ienca et al. 2018: 270-273). US agencies deal with neurotechnologies as weapons as a central priority in new research, resulting in experiments on peripheral nerve stimulation or the assembling of neurons to match animal cortex structures to name a few (Hill 2022: 138, 183ff.).

Even if many neuroscientists express a preference for the open nature of academic research and concurrently position themselves averse to military applications, there is a general approval of military funding if it is framed as *defense*, Kosal and Huang observed. In this regard, government interests and scientific endeavors allow alignment (Kosal and Huang 2015: 105). While security-sensitive research in microbiology, for instance, counts as strictly classified Dual Use Research of Concern (DURC), the neurotechnological axis of it only begun to be viewed as such (Ienca et al. 2018: 269). Similar risks exist for development of genetic weapons because journals would publish dual use techniques internationally and publicly without weighing their security implications (Biberman 2021: 18f.).

Notably, the most advanced researchers in these fields often maintain that there are no limits to the sophisticated tasks their respective technologies can eventually achieve (McCreight 2013: 11-15).

While the technical capability to collect neuro intelligence grows, research is still hindered by methodological limitations. Obtaining samples from a targeted population is a particular challenge – in a military sense this could be useful in active conflicts but realistically hardly to achieve (Bruner and Lentzos 2019: 109f.).

McCreight (2024) highlights the critical need for long-term study of technologies which are designed to deliberately attack human cognition and consequently inform future restrictive programs about it (McCreight 2024: 7ff.).

More than ten years ago, the UK and EU Commission accounted almost 30% of Euro-American funding for synthetic biology. Though the UK's spending was defense-related, other projects refuse to take military funding and want their research to solely rely on non-military and social aspects, Lentzos argues (Lentzos 2016: 58, 61).

Research specifically explores how bioregulators (hormones, cytokines, and neurotransmitters) can be manipulated to cause harmful physiological effects (Nixdorff et al. 2018: 182). DiEuliis (2019) questions whether biotechnology will remain accessible or become a monopoly of well-resourced companies. In any case, increasing the amounts of investment remains critical to maintain future progress (DiEuliis 2019: 134f., 140).

Bruner and Lentzos argue that research has moved from historical programs like the CIA's MKULTRA[13] to modern explorations of genomic-based medicine and synthetic biology (Bruner and Lentzos 2019: 101, 105f., 115). Current efforts deal with the identification of a subject's genetic profile aiming to predict their response to behavioral drugs, which thus would allow states to tailor drug effects (Bruner and Lentzos 2019: 105f.).

Chinese examples of similar bio tech paths can be identified in the China National Genebank, which aims to be the world's largest, and the use of Tianhe supercomputers for processing complex biomedical and genetic information (Kania 2019: 92f.).

Biological weapons are considered less costly to develop than nuclear ones, and there is a strong call for nations to fund research into detection technologies such as SHERLOCK and DETECTR to enhance defensive capabilities of bioweapons (Kosal 2020: 599ff., 614). Current basic and applied research of explorations in specifically somatic and germline editing is limited to basic and applied science (ibid.: 604-608). Regardless, the transnational nature of research and development makes it difficult to control the dissemination of synthetic genomics technology (ibid.: 609, 613) and the inexpensive bioweapons research becomes a borderless, global activity (Cunningham and Geis 2020: 54).

There is a specific need for financing to advance the miniaturization of hardware in the space sector. Research priorities should include developing miniature power control and distribution units, nanoscale energy storage, and

13 MKULTRA was a secret CIA project focusing on mind control via drugs like LSD and so-called truth serums in the 1950s until mid-70s aiming to develop methods for emotional manipulation. Similar paths were also taken by Soviet and Chinese security services (Bruner and Lentzos 2019.: 96).

nano-based computers, according to Concini and Toth (Concini and Toth 2019: 40f.).

For an AI verification regime to be successful, a functional intellectual property annex must be underpinned to protect trade secrets and industry interests. Challenges remain in terms of identifying which specific parts of the CWC model are applicable to AI and whether on-site or remote inspections are feasible in a field defined by cyberspace (Baker 2021: 222f., 224).

Challenges posed by new technologies must be interdisciplinary researched and addressed, while both scientists and citizens play an important role in dealing with the benefits of mutual technological limitations (Altmann 2020: 37-41).

Despite a vast range of research, certain areas are still not addressed. Cultural impacts are not a focus yet. Scenario building might help to direct the path of research and develop roadmaps for improved long-term policy implementation (Frieß et al. 2020: 29, 34). Apart from that, social sciences are often ignored in technical publications in this context (Minvielle et al. 2025: 51). While "the military application of neurotechnology is still in its very early stages – it is less developed than its civilian counterpart and much of the current research is confined to laboratories in a limited number of countries" (Mantellassi and Madziwa 2025: 11), and the field is attracting growing investment and attention. There is a visible transition of advancements from controlled laboratory environments to clinical and viable consumer applications where convergence with other fields is inseparable (ibid.: 7ff., 11). Crucial gaps exist concerning the sociological impacts of these cognitive deception tactics, particularly regarding how trust in public institutions is eroded and how digital algorithm-driven filter bubbles reshape identities of societies and groups within (Marjanović and Smiljanić 2025: 84, 100).

4.1.3 Scenario- and awareness-related assessment

Nordmann anticipated more than 20 years ago, that in a military context, important scenarios involve the use of autonomous fighting robots and the remote manipulation of soldiers' minds (Nordmann 2004: 33f.). Improving the human performance might also end in the transformation of humans into machines (ibid.: 10).

Carafano anticipates future scenarios of warfare in unprecedented levels of asymmetrical warfare, as the gap between military capabilities of economically stronger and weaker states increases (Carafano 2005: 70f.).

Due to the growth of national and international networks, various services are increasingly vulnerable to attacks by criminals and cyber terrorists. Likewise, rapid advances in biotechnology present the scenario of non-state actors gaining access to organisms that have been deliberately modified to cause harm which results in a continuous challenge for global safety (Balakrishnan 2011: 80ff.). Similar threat concerns are expressed by Koblentz (2012): harmful scenarios include natural infectious diseases, laboratory accidents, and deliberate outbreaks caused by states and non-state actors like terrorists (Koblentz 2012: 134ff.). A specific concern involves synthetic genomics, which could allow terrorists to construct dangerous pathogens from scratch, bypassing traditional laboratory biosecurity (ibid.: 143f.). Nevertheless, from a neurotech perspective, Bruner and Lentzos (2019) stress the extreme difficulty to operationalize neuroweapons as they are experimented on in controlled laboratory settings. Historical attempts of MKULTRA failed because the effects of interrogation drugs were too unpredictable and finally not reliably applicable in reality (Bruner and Lentzos 2019: 97, 101).

According to estimations in McCreight's work (2013) by the year 2023, major elements of technology integration and deliberate blending will have already occurred. A turning point in human history through the holistic combination of nanotechnology, biotechnology, information technology, and cognitive science poses another picture of the future. Accordingly, there is a parallel risk of global security erosion if these advancements are not met with strategic oversight (McCreight 2013: 17ff.). Frieß and others (2020) underscore that:

> "scenario-building could serve as an appropriate approach to cover a wide range of potential application cases. Scenario exercises do not claim to make accurate predictions, but rather aim to develop multiple and comparable plausible versions of the contingent future to inform and direct research roadmaps that improve long-term policy planning, and policy implementation" (Frieß et al. 2020: 34).

The concept of mutually assured destruction (MAD) is unlikely to apply because H/nB systems[14] – which include human intelligence – could foresee and prevent countermeasures or duplication attempts. Acting first is incentivized, as the power of H/nB would be so asymmetric, turning future conventional combat between states pointless (Sharp 2020: 334).

Margaret Kosal (2009) sees the most likely scenario in aerosol delivery of nanoparticles containing genetic material such as DNA, RNA, or proteins (Kosal 2009: 91). Plausible scenarios involve the contamination of food and water supplies or the release of lethal nanoparticles within buildings (ibid. 94). Even more futuristic threats could be identified in trigger-like weapons that that remain dormant in the body for years until activated by an external electromagnetic source to destroy tissue (ibid.: 93ff.). Nanotechnology could

14 This refers to neuromorphic BCI (nBCI), which is advanced towards a human-nBCI collaboration possibly being classified as a weapon for an armed attack under the law of going to war (jus ad bellum) (Sharp 2020: 318).

be used to bypass existing vaccines or deliver toxins directly across the blood-brain barrier[15] (BBB) to the central nervous system: Prions or similar proteins could be attached to nano-aerosols capable of crossing the BBB. Prions then could enable unknown applications due to their scientifically evident link to a neurodegenerative disorder called bovine spongiforme enzephalopathie which causes brain tissue to become spongy (ibid.: 91f., 107). Lentzos and Nixdorff and others similarly describe situations of aerosolized dissemination of modified bioregulators over large crowds to induce states like sleep or confusion (Lentzos 2016: 59ff., Nixdorff et al. 2018: 185ff.).

Risk governance in this field is based on forecasting future threats and predicting the potential for bioresearch to be misused. The moratorium of gain-of-function operates as a structure for dual use research as it weighs benefits and potential risks by temporarily pausing scientific research on potentially pathogenic materials (Rychnovská 2016: 316).

Biological agents are particularly dangerous due to their capacity to remain undetected and anonymous, potentially leading to attacks that are difficult to attribute to a specific actor (Kosal 2020).

Other scenarios involve economic warfare via gene drives and the creation of pathogens where simple mail-order DNA could be used – both authors stress that "synthetic biology is inherently dual-use" (Cunningham and Geis 2020: 54f.).

Biberman (2021) describes how actors might use bioweapons (for instance ethnically or individually tailored) overtly against militarily inferior adversaries or democratic states that are sensitive to political fallout (Biberman 2021: 21f.). Crowley and Dando (2023) locate core military interests in toxin and bioregulator weapons which are capable of wide-area battlefield effects, causing mass fatalities or casualties by severely disrupting the CNS and core bodily functions (Crowley and Dando 2023: 15f.).

Beneficial integration of converging neurotech might not be concerning, but more controversial scenarios involve the potential use of non-invasive imaging and stimulation for lie detection and interrogation (Kosal and Huang 2015: 95ff.). Other neurotechnologies like transcranial Direct Current Stimulation (tDCS) could be used to selectively enhance soldiers (Ienca et al. 2018: 269). Gielas (2025) emphasizes potential disruptions of enhancement technology:

> "Explosions and electromagnetic interference could limit or completely disrupt data capture. Other environmental factors such as humidity, extreme temperatures, or physical shocks might impair sensor performance" (Gielas 2025: 10).

15 The BBB serves as the frontier to prevent toxins from entering the central nervous system, yet, nanoparticles can cross the BBB (Kosal 2009: 95).

It seems possible that future threats involve the misuse of riot control tools as neurochemical weapons in war zones and the potential for malicious attacks on Brain-Computer Interfaces (BCI) to extract private information (Ienca et al. 2018: 270ff.). Still, invasive enhancement for healthy individuals seems to remain a distant future scenario due to current safety risks (MacKellar 2019). Halper draws a picture of:

> "Future war [that] will indeed be waged amongst and against the people, with self-directed nanoarmies battling each other and, likely, bypassing each other and attacking humans and their societies directly" (Halper 2015: 109).

In the information space, history demonstrates with events such as the Arab Spring how the political role of technologies and platforms like Twitter/X and Facebook can be unforeseen and tumultuous. Strikes against a nation's technological core from both domestic and foreign actors are possible, necessitating diverse electronic, legal, and military response strategies (Goodman and Khanna 2013: 71ff.). Cyberwar scenarios have transitioned from theory to reality, where state-sponsored attacks like *Stuxnet* and *Flame*[16] would target Iranian infrastructure and computer networks (Halper 2015: 106f.).

Future threats could include actors who may exploit various commercial veiling strategies or practically frame their weaponizable research as defensive and monitoring of comparatively easy-to-develop CRISPR-based[17] elements are hardly monitorable (DeFranco et al. 2019: 52-58). Kosal (2009) expressed these concerns already ten years earlier. Also, scenarios involve the intersection of digital and biological spheres (Kosal 2020: 609ff.) that allow viral particles and proteins from digital DNA sequences to emerge – potentially resulting in biological experiments can be automated and shared rapidly through cloud networks (DeFranco et al. 2019: 52-58). DeFranco, DiEuliis and Giordano (2019) highlight a process of:

> "abstraction [which] could enable biological engineers to simply type in desired features for a biological protein/enzyme, or even an entire microbe, and receive those designs as outputs. In fact, such "computer-generated output" would not even require the engineer to have direct knowledge of the genetic sequences involved" (DeFranco et al. 2019: 54).

16 Stuxnet refers to Stuxnet worm that infiltrated Iran's industrial software that was initial for uranium enrichment infrastructure on behalf of the US and Israel. Flame was a malware for espionage which remained undetected for two to five years on Iranian computers to map networks and monitor computers. The malware also circumvented anti-virus programs (Halper 2015: 106f.).

17 The acronym stands for clustered regularly interspaced short palindromic repeats and works as a kind of genetic scissors. It is often referred to in combination with the Cas9 protein which is responsible for editing the gene sequence (Cunningham and Geis 2020: 52).

In this context, DiEuliis (2019) emphasized *cyberbiosecurity*; security risks should include such vulnerabilities. Concerning futures might entail the sabotage of biotech products that become part of critical infrastructure and the potential for adversaries to use biotechnology for human degradation. Agency and accessibility are additional points of future risk assessments (DiEuliis 2019: 131-139).

Since there are few historical high-technology battles, simulations could become the primary method for preparing for and modelling future combat scenarios with e.g., reduced decision-making time due to automation (Altmann 2020: 39ff.). A similar idea can be found in recommendations for strategic wargaming to address future scenarios with non-kinetic attacks (Eads et al. 2023: 5, 18). Regarding automated decision making, Mantellassi and Madziwa stress the risk of obscuring the line between human judgement and algorithms (Mantellassi and Madziwa 2025: 19, 23f.).

As Hill (2022), Hensing and Schlecht (2025) emphasize, future situations could be characterized by drone warfare where pilot brains are wirelessly linked to video-vision systems, creating a system of mind-controlled drones (Hill 2022: 137, Hensing and Schlecht 2025: 15).

Facial recognition technology (FRT) is being deployed in reconnaissance and targeting operations. The Israel Defense Forces (IDF) have integrated FRTs and AI-powered systems like *Lavender* for identity verification at checkpoints. They were also used to assist targeting in Gaza. Deploying such technologies in uncontrolled environments shaped by dust or poor lighting and even civilians nearby, crucially risks misidentification and violations of international humanitarian law (Bromley and Maletta 2025: 7ff.).

It seems like that actors could engage in covert misuse by subtly altering a nanoparticle's shape or surface properties to transform it from a non-toxic substance into a toxic weapon (Nixdorff et al. 2018: 185f.).

A specific scenario of concern from Bosch and Ham (2007) involves the potential compromise of scientists or engineers due to the knowledge they possess of WMD weaponization and specialized or dual use technology processes. They might be forced or coerced to aid criminal or terrorist objectives (Bosch and van Ham 2007: 215). Scenarios involving CBRN crisis management distinguish between military force protection in the international arena and civilian-led domestic responses. They must be considered for adequate preparation of response and recovery phases in which security and safety become blurry often. Generally, the threat universe is broadening, and capabilities require urgent action (Frinking et al. 2009: 79f.).

Neuroscientific applications are envisioned for several specific scenarios, including the reduction of information-processing burdens for warfighters to help them identify visual targets on a battlefield more quickly. Within the military, situations involving remote brain control or required medical interventions for duty fitness raise significant concerns regarding autonomous freedom (Tennison and Moreno 2012: 2). Hayes and Cavazos see potential military scenarios to entail forward-deployed conventional forces that are smaller and faster, making them much more difficult for local conventional or nuclear weapons to target (Hayes and Cavazos 2015: 263). Apart from this scenario, massive urbanization is highlighted as a primary driver that could render the use of weapons of mass destruction against specific places and people logically and strategically indefensible (ibid.: 317). By the middle of the century, the authors anticipated that there will be a global awareness of the absurdity of nuclear weapons and state-based nuclear deterrence strategies (ibid.). Regarding offensive neurowarfare, potentials:

> "could also mean collapsing adversarial states by creating conditions of lawlessness, insurrection, and revolution, for example, by inducing fear, confusion, or anger. Adversarial states could be destabilized using advanced techniques of subversion, sabotage, environmental modification, and 'gray' terrorism, followed by a direct military attack. […] Neurowarfare could take down a strategic competitor permanently without nuclear war and the risk of devastating nuclear retaliation" (Krishnan 2016: 17f.).

Krishnan describes military scenarios including the use of neurohormones like oxytocin to manipulate adversaries into temporarily trusting forces to reduce resistance. In the past, the investigation of so-called *gay bombs* was pursued by US military aiming to distract enemy forces through sexual distraction and disrupted morale. Deceiving people to believe they already lost or won could also end hostilities prematurely (Krishnan 2016: 11f, 17). On the battlefield, deploying neurobiochemical weapons (NBCW) faces essential challenges because it is nearly impossible to ensure that a broad population would receive a dosage sufficient enough to influence behavior without being lethal (Bruner and Lentzos 2019). McCreight (2024) underlines:

> "the sheer magnitude and interactive complexity of these convergently engineered technologies [that create] a widely unknown degree of risk and possible misuse by those engaged in doing so" (McCreight 2024: 7).

From a Chinese perspective, possible futures are shaped by command being exercised via brain-machine integration and supported by cloud infrastructure (Kania 2019: 83f.). The battlefield is expected to expand into the biological domain (生物疆域) where the weaponization of living organisms and unconventional combat styles become a new reality (ibid.: 90f.). Weaker militaries might even find an advantage in scenarios which involve operations to subvert and counter an adversary's capabilities (逆智能化) (ibid.: 85f.).

In the space domain, future scenarios make use of nano-medicine to enhance the human immune system against radiation and deploying nanorobotics that utilize swarm intelligence for complex operations (Concini and Toth 2019: 40).

4.1.4 Technological assessment

Technological advancement is currently driven by biotechnology and bioinformatics, which are shaping the character of war in ways that may exceed public control. These technologies offer the potential to reshape medical practices and enhance human performance, allowing for individual achievement and endurance levels previously unseen. However, the dual-use nature of these technical skills and equipment increases the risk that they will be repurposed for biological weaponry (Carafano 2005: 68).

McCreight (2013) stresses that the technological landscape is defined by the convergence of genomics, proteomics, synthetic biology, cybernetics, AI, neuroscience, and also robotics. This involves the collaboration of cyber systems with AI and the merging of robotics with nanobiological research. Specific areas of focus include nanobiotechnology, nanomedicine, nanoelectronics, and nanophotonics, though researchers must account for the significant limitations and constraints imposed by the environment of space (McCreight 2013: 11-19). Goodman and Khanna (2013) likewise emphasize the wide range of tech and particularly highlight geotechnology and its link to biotechnology.

McCreight (2024) additionally introduces scalar wave technology, which consists of non-linear waves that propagate faster than light and can modulate biochemical communication between nerve cells (McCreight 2024: 3-7). Vicariously for other technological innovations, he states in the context of electromagnetic fields (EMF):

> "EMF radiation is persuasively reported to affect the CNS, brain chemistry, and histology and traverses the blood-brain barrier. We lack better evidence to ascertain what the biophysical and neurological impact of EMF on human life really indicates or implies" (McCreight 2024: 6).

FRTs facilitate facial detection, facial analysis (such as gender perception), and identification through verification (Bromley and Maletta 2025: 5). The Software as a Service model, where software is accessed via cloud computing rather than physical downloads, complicates traditional oversight additionally (ibid.: 10f.).

Nanotechnology is characterized by its broad application across human activities and its ability to facilitate dispersed production (Balakrishnan 2011: 85). In biotechnology, genetic engineering now allows for the transfer of genetic material across species, including between plants and animals, and even the insertion of synthetic genes into life forms. Meanwhile, the development of information technology has necessitated the creation of complex technical measures to combat cybercrime (ibid.: 81ff.).

Gold and silver nanoparticles are being engineered to enhance signal strength in spectroscopies like Raman scattering, which helps to overcome the low signal levels typically associated with remote detection (Kosal 2009: 46-49). However, technical challenges remain, such as difficulties in quality control for nanowire assembly and the non-specificity of some nanomaterials to chemical agents (ibid.: 50-53). Human Performance Enhancement would be steadily built via bionics, brain-computer devices, genetic engineering, and drugs with the aim to alter perceptions (Halper 2015: 108, 110).

Technological progress has enabled the use of nanoparticles under 100 nm to bypass the immune system using stealth strategies. To cross the above-mentioned BBB, researchers utilize lipophilic carriers or modify particles to target overexpressed receptors, such as insulin receptors (Nixdorff et al. 2018: 183f.). Additionally, the formation of a biocorona – a surface coating – allows nanoparticles to absorb neurotoxic proteins. The absorption rate of nano particles is of considerable advantage. As nanoparticles can be transformed from non-toxic to toxic (via shape, size, surface properties), this can be viewed as a covert nanoparticle misuse potential (ibid.: 187).

MacKellar categorized the neuro innovations by input, output, and feedback loop systems (MacKellar 2019: 47ff.). These range from non-invasive neuroimaging (EEG, fMRI) to invasive implants like deep brain stimulation or even neural mesh. The author describes additionally the functioning of RAM[18] which seeks to facilitate the formation of memories on one hand and the retrieval of existing memories on the other (ibid.: 83ff.).

Pharmaceutical enhancements are also prominent due to their featuring of substances like modafinil for cognitive enhancement in sleep-deprived individuals and orexin-A to restore short-term memory. Additionally, fMRI is being explored for its potential in brain-reading and lie detection. Brain-brain-interfaces that provide sensory feedback, BCIs, brain scanning, neuromodulation or optogenetics are furthermore of relevance in this context (Tennison and Moreno 2012: 1ff.). For the widely discussed BCIs, Ienca, Jotterand and Elger (2018) observe that:

> "even though there are no confirmed cases of malicious attacks in non-experimental settings, information security researchers have experimentally demonstrated the actual feasibility of performing side-channel attacks and extracting private information from users of EEG-based BCIs without their authorization" (Ienca et al. 2018: 270).

18 Restoring Active Memory

Kosal and Huang (2015) also deal with sophisticated tools such as functional magnetic resonance imaging (fMRI), near-infrared spectroscopy (NIRS), and transcranial magnetic stimulation (TMS) (Kosal and Huang 2015: 96). These techniques allow for noninvasive imaging and brain stimulation. While tools like fMRI can measure changes in blood flow as a proxy for brain activation, their use for mind-reading or predicting complex behaviors like patriotism through activity in certain brain regions is still nascent and limited (Bruner and Lentzos 2019: 97, 109f.). Despite the many interfaces and novel technologies in neuroscience, the gap of specific safeguards against malicious hacking of medical neuromodulation devices and neuroimaging-based interrogation has also been discussed (Ienca et al. 2018: 270. 272). Brain-brain networks would currently be limited by low data transfer bit rates and the requirement for invasive surgical probes to stimulate deep regions of the brain, Bruner and Lentzos describe (Bruner and Lentzos 2019: 107). H/nB utilizes neuromorphic chips that mimic human thought, allowing real-time adjustments in dynamic combat situations. These systems trigger synaptic plasticity and neurochemical releases to expedite learning, enhance spatial navigation, and improve threat recognition, potentially equipping humans nearly unlimited cognitive capabilities (Sharp 2020: 322, 329ff.). Innovations also lie in the Diffusion Tension Imaging (DTI) and fast-acting algorithms that surpass standard medical MRIs (Hill 2022: 177).

A key feature of cognitive intelligence that Conde and Whiskeyman mention (COGINT) is that data collection often occurs through everyday technology interactions without the individual's conscious awareness (Conde and Whiskeyman 2025: 12). AI and machine learning drive COGINT by collecting biometric signatures and digital behavioral signals from personal devices (ibid.: 4, 18). They note that:

> "advances in cognitive psychology and computational neuroanalytics now make it possible to interrogate the neural and psychometric substrates of cognition—linking personality traits, affective states, and decision heuristics to measurable behavioral outputs" (ibid.: 5).

NeuroStrike involves the covert use of radio frequency (RF), nanotech, and electromagnetic technologies to inflict permanent neurological damage. Additionally, nightless drugs or sleep-inducing tech as well as soft-kill radio waves are mentioned by Eads and others (2023). These tools offer a direct link between the human brain and external devices, allowing a physiological manipulation of behavior and emotion (Eads et al. 2023: 5, 12f.). Applications also range from sensing brain activity for behavioral adjustments to connecting the brain to virtual reality and augmenting memory or communication (Hensing and Schlecht 2025: 12f.,15f.).

Other developments are explained by Krishnan (2016). They involve implanted chips for drug release, Directed Energy Weapons (DEWs) such as microwaves that can disrupt the nervous system, and mind-controlling parasites that can modify behavior by switching genes on or off (Krishnan 2016: 7f., 12f.). Beyond that, defense establishments are developing invisibility cloaks and holograms to create illusions on the battlefield (Krishnan 2016: 14).

Altmann (2020) also underscores developments like hypersonic missiles, autonomous weapons, and additive manufacturing, which can support biological weapons programs. Digital advancements like deep neural networks and cyber weapons are particularly problematic because they can be more or less easily multiplied and kept secret until use (Altmann 2020: 39). He emphasizes:

> "turning from espionage to attack is easy. Attribution to the real originator is difficult. The opacity of machine learning, in particular with deep neural networks[19], has led to calls for explainable AI. The USA, Russia and China see AI as a major component of their future military strength, by incorporating more information and enabling faster action" (ibid.).

The general trend involves smaller systems and easier access to sophisticated technology, which increases the risks of hacking and deception (ibid.: 39ff.).

Synthetic genomics allows scientists to construct infectious viruses using nucleotide strands ordered from commercial providers. Because these innovations are increasingly available on a global basis it seems unrealistic to truly prevent their proliferation. Efforts to develop safeguards are ongoing within the private sector, but technological standards are not yet uniform (Koblentz 2012: 143f.). Technologies enable the production of new opioids and toxins, as well as the creation of bio-based materials like *dragon silk* for military applications (DiEuliis 2019: 130f., 138).

Synthetic biology remains confounding, Lentzos argues, as standardizing and mechanizing these processes is a major challenge. Practical application still requires specialized training in techniques like ligation and cloning, which cannot be reduced to trivial instructions (Lentzos 2016: 55ff.). While hurdles remain regarding weaponizability of biotech, delivery, and its precision, overcoming them is viewed as a matter of time. Genetic agents can achieve unprecedented specificity which was impossible with traditional pathogens (Biberman 2021: 18f.).

The field of biological big data (biodata) enables DNA mining and computer experimentation. Innovations like robotic automation and computational algorithms (e.g. CRISPOR, CHOPCHOP) have made genetic modification faster and more affordable through accurate guiding RNA (DeFranco et al. 2019: 53f.).

19 Neural Networks are core elements of Deep Learning and AI as they provide the basis for applications such as voice and facial recognition or language to text adaptation to model the human brain's learning aptitude (Rashid 2024).

Crowley and Dando (2023) add to this with the convergence of neuroscience, AI, and synthetic biology enabling the development of a multi-faceted system of warfare agents. In the past, research successfully identified components from ten different plants that can simultaneously target the nervous, cardiac, and respiratory systems. Studies evaluate the potential of natural bio-threat agents, such as highly toxic aconitine, to serve as lethal or less lethal weapons. These assessments explore the potential for formulating future agents by experimenting with stinging plants (Crowley and Dando 2023: 12f.).

Key breakthroughs in East Asia include a chip that enables brain-talk, a brain-computer chip designed to decode neural electrical signals with high precision and speed. The Chinese People's Liberation Army (PLA) has also invested over 20 years into brain-machine interfaces (脑机接口), enabling the neural operation of robots, vehicles, and computers. China simultaneously pursues CRISPR gene-editing technology, viewing it as a disruptive tool where China must grasp the initiative, and is exploring the concept of *brain networking* (脑联网) to enhance battlefield communication (Kania 2019: 87-93).

Overall, challenges remain: technical limitations include the degradation of components due to brain biology and the still incomplete understanding of the human brain (Mantellassi and Madziwa 2025: 9f.).

4.1.5 *Ethical assessment*

In the early 2000s, ethical concerns regarding the engineering of mind and body occurred, also because of the invisibility of converging tech and the potential for complacency induced by the perceived potential of technology to solve nearly all problems. As a result, these innovations would likely exacerbate the separation of rich and poor as well as those who are technologically advanced and those who are not (Nordmann 2004: 6-9). Specific ethical issues include the manipulation of soldiers to prevent sleep deprivation and the broader risk of transhumanism undermining human nature (ibid.: 34).

For Kosal (2009), the primary ethical concern is the dual use nature of nanotechnology, where almost all equipment and materials for beneficial research can be inverted for hostile purposes, protecting from and deterring malicious actors will mean bridging communication gaps between scientists and operators, and building dialogue among the intelligence, policy, and economics fields (Kosal 2009: 90f., 129). Ethicists emphasize that scientist engagement is necessary to address the ramifications of dual use research. Some scholars argue for a risk-benefit analysis or type of smart regulation over a strictly precautionary approach, noting that the hazards of emerging technologies often cannot be accurately evaluated a priori (Kosal and Huang 2015: 96, 105).

There is an ethical imperative to educate life scientists on the risks that their research knowledge could be misused for harmful purposes (Lentzos 2016: 61ff.). This process redefines the principles of scientific responsibility, turning ethical frameworks into tools for security management. However, this *ethicalization* can change the criteria for the validity of knowledge, altering how scientists produce truth claims and reflect on their own work (Rychnovská 2016: 310, 323). Preventive assessments must also evaluate whether these technologies cause undue harm to humans or the environment during peacetime (Altmann 2020: 37).

Lack of transparency may undermine the capacity for innovative Chinese technologies to be adopted on a global scale, as international partners remain skeptical of the underlying systems (Kania 2021: 18). More broadly speaking, concerns involve the lack of public consultation and prior informed consent in current application practices (Frieß et al. 2020: 29ff.). Coupling the public sector participation, McCreight (2013) identifies a lack of serious public debate regarding converging technology (McCreight 2013: 3).

As the dual use potential is inherent in modern biotechnology; its success would rely on addressing this issue within a road-map for policy-makers and to bridge health and security communities in order to secure global health (Koblentz 2012: 148). Regarding dual use risks, some experts belittle the subtle threats of these technologies, viewing their potential nefarious use as minimally dangerous (McCreight 2013: 15). Secrecy within defense establishments regarding toxins and bioregulatory pathways generates significant social and ethical disquiet, especially as their development is coming near the line or even crossing it in terms of offensive weapons research (Crowley and Dando 2023: 12).

The potential to use tools like CRISPR/Cas9 or synthetic drugs to induce selective brain malfunctions, such as a total loss of emotion or memory, poses a grave threat to human autonomy (Nixdorff et al. 2018: 185, 190ff.). The potential to alter a person's memories, identity, or sacred beliefs raises profound ethical questions regarding the violation of individual autonomy (Bruner and Lentzos 2019: 109f.). Despite these concerns, the non-lethal label attached to neuroweapons and neurobiochemical threats may actually encourage their use sooner rather than later (Bruner and Lentzos 2019: 108). concerns are primarily centered on germline editing, which aims to change inheritable DNA passed to future generations. There are also significant risks regarding unwanted edits in genes, which could unintentionally lead to conditions like leukaemia. The intersection of gene editing and cognitive neurosciences raises the controversial possibility of human enhancement, such as altering memory and cognition. These developments challenge existing norms regarding the boundaries of clinical biomedical research (Kosal 2020: 604ff.).

Military neurotechnology should be non-coercive, ensuring that individuals retain their cognitive liberty – the right to refuse brain-altering devices. To manage these risks, the sources advocate for codes of ethical conduct and individual obligations, such as the 2010 pledge for neuroscientists to refuse participation in applications that violate human rights (Ienca et al. 2018: 272f.). A primary ethical discussed concern by Tennison and Moreno (2012) is the risk of coercion, which is more pronounced in the military where soldiers may be required to accept invasive interventions like remote brain control to stay fit for duty. Moreover, the potential use of neurotechnology to detect deception or manipulate virtues like trust and sacrifice through hormones like oxytocin creates lots of ethical concerns. Some argue for a complete divorce between the sciences and the military, though others believe the dual-use possibilities make such a separation unlikely (Tennison and Moreno 2012: 2f.). Major ethical concerns include the privacy of brain decoding and the risk-benefit ratio of enhancement. There are also significant risks regarding reversibility and long-term vascular damage from implants (MacKellar 2019). In a corresponding way, concerns about the permanent manipulation of body, mind, and mood came up. A central ethical challenge is the reduction of human control as warfare speeds up beyond human intervention capabilities (Altmann 2020: 39ff.). Neurotechnology is uniquely sensitive because it directly impacts consciousness, autonomy, identity, and the fundamental human experience (Hensing and Schlecht 2025:3f., 6). Conde and Whiskeyman (2025) similarly address the protection of cognitive sovereignty and privacy, as these operations exploit subconscious decision-making processes (Conde and Whiskeyman 2025: 19ff.). Concerns center on the informed consent of soldiers and their right to refuse enhancement (Mantellassi and Madziwa 2025: 20, 22f.)

It also appears risky to receive false positives, which can lead to wrongful arrests, misidentification, and the violation of privacy rights (Bromley and Maletta 2025: 8). There are documented risks of FRTs being used for the systematic repression of ethnic minorities, such as the Uyghurs in China (Bromley and Maletta 2025: 9).

4.1.6 *Legal assessment*

Despite domestic legal structures, international nonproliferation efforts are expected to have a difficult time keeping pace with the rapid expansion of the global biotechnology industry (Carafano 2005: 68f.). There is an international push for the universal adoption of WMD treaties because technologies related to biological and chemical weapons are becoming increasingly accessible, Bosch and van Ham observe in 2007 (Bosch and van Ham 2007: 218f.). However, because every country has a unique legal system and culture, it remains unclear if models of cooperation will be effective or compatible across different global legal structures. Additionally, many states currently lack the capacity to enforce complex legislation or export control systems (Bosch and van Ham 2007: 217ff.). Closing export loopholes and implementing sanctions against firms that violate technology transfer strictures must be addressed. Strategies are needed to shape legal responses regarding attacks from actors that are less traceable than traditional states. There is also a critique of current legal-political frameworks, noting that a *sovereignty first approach* may overestimate the real control states actually exert over technological flows (Goodman and Khanna 2013: 71ff.). Hayes and Cavazos mention cross-border integrative processes driven by the globalization of culture, economy, and technology. These processes contribute to the transformation of the international system, moving it away from the state-based frameworks that previously defined nuclear deterrence strategies (Hayes and Cavazos 2015: 278, 317).

Global bans on military neuroscience research were in the past proposed by the European Parliament to prevent the manipulation of human beings through brain-related weapons (Ienca et al. 2018). Furthermore, there is a historical reluctance to trigger challenge mechanisms in existing treaties like the CWC, potentially due to a silent agreement to avoid tit-for-tat escalations, meaning these mechanisms remain untested for AI contexts (Baker 2021: 220f.). Baker also states that:

> "the CWC is a more viable regime than the BWC, in part, because ongoing review conferences adjust and update the chemical schedules. Thus, the text is not locked in a moment in technological time" (Baker 2021: 223).

An important research gap remains in finding more effective technological governance and the specific role neuroscientists should play in formulating these policies (Kosal and Huang 2015: 94-98). The convergence of scientific fields also complicates arms control, as new weapons may fall between existing legal jurisdictions (Lentzos 2016: 48f., 61f, Krishnan 2016: 18f.). The CWC contains a loophole regarding riot control agents that could be co-opted for offensive neurochemical – or even neurobiochemical threats for law enforcement (Bruner and Lentzos 2019: 112, 116). There is an urgent need for evolutive interpretation of human rights to protect mental privacy and integrity, as existing legal frameworks fall into a *regulatory chasm* regarding the mental dimension of neurotechnology (Ienca et al. 2018: 271ff.). Likewise, DeFranco et al. (2019) and Nixdorff et al. (2018) underline the weaknesses of the BWC and CWC, also Cunningham and Geis (2020). Existing list-based security paradigms are increasingly viewed as insufficient for modern threats, necessitating new international governance structures (DiEuliis 2019: 130-133). Integrating biotechnology into defense also requires navigating liability issues and establishing specific acquisition requirements for new materials (DiEuliis 2019: 134, 138).

A major legal challenge is the difficulty in distinguishing defensive nanotechnology programs from offensive ones, which complicates verification efforts under the Biological and Toxin Weapons Convention. Effective nonproliferation policy must involve updating legal schedules to include new precursors at the intersection of chemistry, biology, and nanotechnology (Kosal 2009: 128). Kosal and Putney (2022) observe that such new technologies "may problematize offense-defense theory by challenging the distinction between offensive and defensive weapons" (Kosal and Putney 2022: 83).

A *no-first-use doctrine* is being discussed by Krishnan (2016) and should be applied to offensive neurowarfare (Krishnan 2016: 18f.). While H/nB weapons must undergo Law of Armed Conflict reviews – no specific international laws currently prohibit attacks delivered through combined data and thought. Nonetheless, current legal standards do not fully contemplate a warfighter serving simultaneously as a weapon (Sharp 2020: 327f., 337).

In fields such as electromagnetics, cyber, and nanotechnology, there are currently no real boundaries or rules of conduct. This lack of governance makes it nearly impossible to regulate or restrict the development of technologies designed to impair human neurobiological health (McCreight 2024: 8ff.). This is why concerns also center on the protection of neural data, the regulation of supply chain risks, and the application of existing EU regulations to this dynamic field. There is an urgent need to clarify how current laws apply to neurotech to reduce obstacles to research while advancing cybersecurity and data protection (Hensing and Schlecht 2025: 42f.).

There is a profound lack of policy, doctrine, and strategy to address the ripening of metatechnologies (McCreight 2013: 19). Global powers will potentially compete to put their own identity on the control and evolution of these technologies, suggesting an absence of unified international legal frameworks or shared regulatory standards (McCreight 2013: 13ff.). The dominant state utilizes bilateral and multilateral enforcement tools to protect its preferred rules and practices. Underdeveloped, domain-specific rules lead to hegemonic activity to lead efforts in creating new legal norms, such as those against economically motivated cyber espionage. Over time, rising states are expected to implement stronger internal enforcement of intellectual property laws as they acquire more of their own technology (Kennedy and Lim 2018: 571f.). A notable milestone in this context was the 2015 agreement between the U.S. and China, where both pledged not to support the theft of trade secrets for commercial advantage (Kennedy and Lim 2018: 568ff.).

Traditional arms control agencies, modelled after Cold War-era nuclear verification, are increasingly viewed as inadequate for securing emerging biological technologies. There is a pressing need for international agreements that eliminate legal routes for actors to obtain precursors or weaponization materials (Kosal 2020: 609ff.). Legal issues, such as the *posse comitatus* act in the United States, act as a barrier to the efficient allocation and division of capabilities between military and civilian actors (Frinking et al. 2009: 68, 79).

The legal framework in the EU is anchored in export controls like the Wassenaar Arrangement – which "is focused on preventing the proliferation and misuse of conventional arms" (Bromley and Maletta 2025: 9) – and the EU Dual-Use Regulation (ibid.: 9, 12). However, many FRTs currently fall into a legal vacuum, as they are often excluded from specific control lists or defined in ways that exempt overt surveillance (ibid.: 8ff, 12f.). The authors argue that:

> "to fully address risks of misuse and diversion, export controls will need to be complemented by other soft-law instruments, such as requiring companies to embed human rights due diligence processes in the conduct of their business" (ibid. 2025: 2).

Moreover, the militarization of technology is complicated by overall tensions: Russia for instance has reportedly used its veto power within the mentioned Wassenaar Arrangement to block new export controls on emerging technologies (Bromley and Maletta 2025: 10, 15).

4.1.7 Psychological assessment

Cognitive science is a core component of NBIC convergence, and research is required to understand the implications of remote mind manipulation and the psychological effects of body manipulation in high-stress environments like the battlefield (Nordmann 2004: 33f.). Caduff (2008) stresses that the lack of clear definitions for dangerous research leads to a threat of intervention as very present (Caduff 2008: 272f.).

Institutional implementation of revolutionary technology is often blocked by skepticism, limited recognition, and an open averseness toward farsighted technological concepts. These non-technical barriers are as crucial as the technical ones and must be overcome to realize future defense goals. Resolving programmatic and institutional issues pose a key challenge in coordinating chemical and biological defense efforts (Kosal 2009: 121, 125ff.).

There is another concern regarding social equilibrium, a psychological pressure where individuals are not formally coerced but feel compelled to use neuroenhancements to avoid being at a significant disadvantage compared to peers (Ienca et al. 2018: 272f.). Soldier enhancements could involve reversible or irreversible changes to mental states, affecting soldiers' psyches (Altmann 2020: 40f.). Genetic weapons are exemplary tools for intimidation and outbidding, particularly for weaker states attempting to influence others (Biberman 2021: 21f.). Cyberwarfare is increasingly implemented within psychological warfare, including the dissemination of disinformation and propaganda to populations via the internet (Halper 2015: 106). Psychological assessments in a security context explore human engineering and behavior, specifically where they seek to predict and enhance the cognitive performance of warfighters. The research also delves into the attitudes of researchers themselves, finding that their perceptions of whether research is *offensive* or *defensive* substantially influences their willingness to participate in security-related projects (Kosal and Huang 2015: 94f.).

Research into the gut-brain axis suggests that even covertly altering a person's diet could manipulate the neurochemistry underlying their behavior and stress response. Taking this knowledge into account, psychological operations might leverage these biological markers to design propaganda that is more likely to trigger desired emotional responses in a target group (Bruner and Lentzos 2019: 104, 109f.). In general, neurotechnology entails the ability to influence mood, emotions, and cognitive processes, as well as reduce undesired sensations like pain (Hensing and Schlecht 2025: 15f.). It is being investigated for its ability to modulate alertness and improve resilience against physical and cognitive stress in military contexts (Hensing and Schlecht 2025: 31f., 35).

Military neuroscience targets cognitive nonconsciousness, or the *unthought* which refers to cognitive processes inaccessible to a subject's conscious introspection but accessible to machines. By using neural prosthetics, the military seeks to bypass the psyche altogether, focusing instead on working memory and the electrochemical functioning of synapses (Hill 2022: 175, 184ff). In the Chinese view, success on the future battlefield is tied to achieving *mental/cognitive dominance* (制脑权) (Kania 2019: 85). This involves military *perception confrontation* (军事感知对抗), which uses physiological, psychological, and technical means to hinder or distort an adversary's cognition and undermine their will to fight. The PLA is exploring the use of performance-enhancing drugs like Modafinil and leveraging brain science to exploit inherent vulnerabilities in human cognition to manipulate enemy decision-making (Kania 2019: 87). Psychological strategies aim to create *cognitive fog* (认知迷雾) and establish *mental anchors* (心锚) to subtly influence minds (Eads et al. 2023: 8f.).

4.1.8 Theoretical assessment

Traditional military frameworks, specifically Clausewitz's principles of war, are increasingly viewed as anachronistic and counterproductive in the 21st century. These principles of war are seen as a burden when adjusting to the challenges of asymmetrical and private-sector involvement (Carafano 2005: 70f.). The shifting away from Clausewitz is likewise emphasized by Krishnan (2016). The focus moves away from physical violence and towards *neocortical warfare*, which views the brain as the primary target. This paradigm suggests that the real object of war is subduing the enemy's will. Neurowarfare is theoretically similar to cyber warfare, but instead of attacking technical networks, it targets biological cognitive systems through neuro-cyber interfaces (Krishnan 2016: 15f.).

Caduff (2008) distinguishes between biosafety (accidental risk) and biosecurity (deliberate abuse of information) (Caduff 2008: 258f.). The boundary between safe and dangerous research is not fixed, making the potential for regulatory oversight limitless (Caduff 2008: 272). Frinking and others similarly include examining the division between security and safety, especially during the response and recovery phases of a crisis, to determine if the current separation of these concepts remains functional (Frinking et al. 2009: 79).

Theoretical models of state-based nuclear deterrence are described as becoming obsolete due to the integrative processes of globalization (Hayes and Cavazos 2015: 278, 317). Kosal therefore calls for effective deterrence in this field to require a theoretical bridge between life sciences and social sciences. Furthermore, any credible regime must be structured to acknowledge and absorb high levels of uncertainty to remain effective against evolving threats (Kosal 2020: 612f.).

Apart from that, there are discussions on identifying a bidirectional character of dual use, where civilian and military developments constantly spill over into one another. To address this, a new theoretical *neurosecurity framework* is proposed, which adapts established biosecurity strategies from other life sciences to the specific challenges of neuroscience (Ienca et al. 2018: 271f.). Ienca and others state that the "neurosecurity framework could help anticipate future threats and maximize security in the neurotechnology domain through calibrated regulatory interventions, (neuro) ethical codes of conduct, and awareness-raising activities across the scientific community and the public" (ibid.: 273).

It is necessary to mention that theoretically, any biochemical molecule can be weaponized if its delivery is sufficiently controlled (Nixdorff et al. 2018: 181-196).

Theoretical challenges are located in the need for a clear definition of neuroweapons to formulate effective countermeasures (DeFranco et al. 2019: 59f.). The emergence of sociogenomics and cyberbiosecurity requires new theoretical frameworks to address how neurobiological manipulation can be used in sociopolitical contexts to coerce or control populations (DeFranco et al. 2019: 54ff.). As prior underlined, the emerging cyberbiosecurity fuses cybersecurity and biosecurity and is needed to protect the digital infrastructure supporting synthetic biology. This theoretical shift treats biology as a multidisciplinary domain where digital data and physical pathogens are interconnected (Cunningham and Geis 2020: 58). The CWC could serve as a superior analogy for AI regulation because it includes a functional verification regime for dual use capacity. Still, it remains a theoretical question whether a regime designed for physical chemical schedules can be successfully mapped onto cyberspace (Baker 2021: 222f.).

Cognitive warfare is an emerging theoretical concept that focuses on the integration of techno-social engineering and cognitive strategies. Marjanović and Smiljanić observe that "neither the military nor the academic community has established a fully developed concept of Cognitive Warfare" (Marjanović and Smiljanić 2025: 87f.). A robust framework would involve mapping Technology Readiness Levels to military utility to distinguish between obvious foresight and advanced research. Meaningful foresight requires a relational approach rather than isolated technological analysis (Minvielle et al. 2025: 29, 51).

4.2 Synthesis and Discussion

Recalling the element of utmost importance in ILR, the "synthesis is a creative process that integrates existing ideas with new ideas to develop new perspectives on the topic" (Torraco 2016: 409). Consequently, the assessment types from chapter 4 were integrated into a model which will be described in the following as part of the synthesis.

4.2.1 The NBIC Weaponization Cycle

This model shows a possible visualization of the weaponization process that NBIC converging technologies underlie, based on the literature review conducted. As was attributed to the statistician George Box "all models are wrong, but some are useful" (Ricklin 2025), this cycle does not aim to be definite. It rather shows the potential integration of respective developments at each point – adding the scholarly focus from selected literature of the review. Additionally, the conceptual structuring of chapter 3.3 was integrated by highlighting those areas touched upon by modern warfare characteristics in a context of dual use NBIC convergence. Here, multiple domains are touched, including cyber and the most recent attention-seeking cognitive domain. The relevance of non-state actors, especially in the light of terrorism, was clearly demonstrated. Blurring lines between combatants and civilians depict an unpleasant, yet real change in battlefields. With political objectives to maintain or gain power, the role of force is downscaled respectively – attempting to operate below the threshold of military war.

As the cycle displays, there is no exact beginning of the weaponizing process. However, a relatable start could be the doctrine/strategy box. Here, political and strategic views must be taken into account when technological deterrence, defense or offensive mechanisms are the objective for states. Likewise, non-state actors and their respective strategy come into play following the same logic. Financial resources are allocated for research and development to reach the next milestone: the factual development of dual use applications. These are obtainable by states and non-state actors.

As the star (*) in the figure 2 indicates, the technological development is further characterized by complementing the dual use understanding over time. Figure 3 demonstrates this change. Over time it shifts and, in terms of technological convergence, the classical civil military understanding becomes less central. Moreover, another point is added implicitly by scholars questioning the useful- and harmfulness of technologies rather than questioning their applicability and origin in civil or military spheres. It does not intend to completely replace the traditional divide but to add it as yet another point worth noting in this regard.

Technological development obviously needs technological assessments, which here are followed by ethical and legal considerations of NBIC convergences-to-be. The latter ones frame the technological deployment.

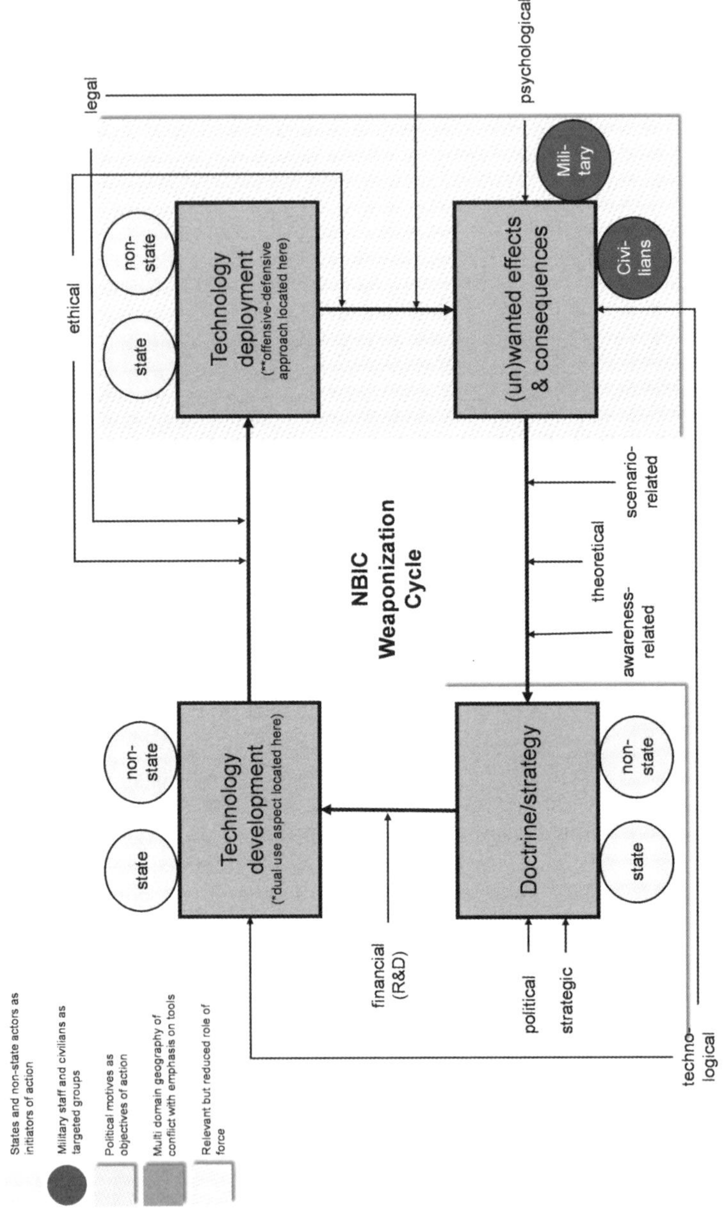

Figure 2: NBIC Weaponization Cycle, own figure.

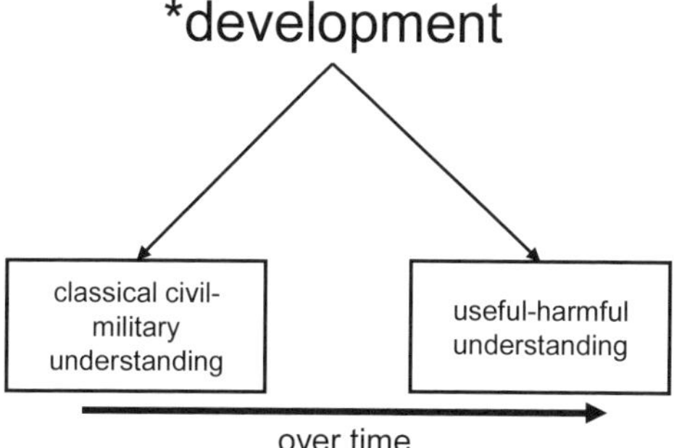

Figure 3: Implicit dual use understanding over time, own figure.

At this point, the approach of dividing weaponry into defensive and offensive applications is located. After the review of articles, scholars discuss the deployment of NBIC technologies gradually under the circumstances of overt use on one side and covert use on the other. Figure 4 demonstrates this division. This might anticipate a paradigmatic change in future weapon deployment in converging technology.

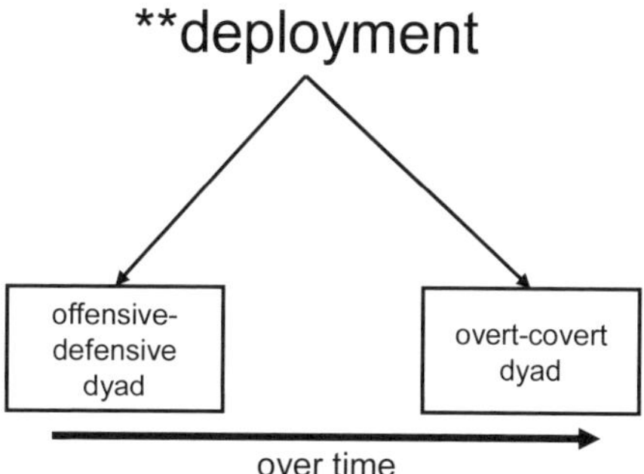

Figure 4: Offensive-defensive approach over time, own figure.

Technological assessments also become relevant at the point of real-life consequences and effects, given that there is a certain potential for unwanted outcomes. These effects are intended to target – and harm or enhance – primarily civilians and military personnel (rather than nature as an example). Scenario- and awareness-related assessments stand between effects/consequences and doctrine/strategy, the same is true for theoretical considerations. They entail risk assessments and evaluations of past and upcoming innovations and can be imagined taking effect at probably any other point in the cycle. Finally, the cycle starts from new.

4.2.2 The weaponized NBIC convergence map

The Weaponized NBIC convergence cycle identifies the most present assessments within the selected data set and assigned them to specific spots within a process of weaponization, backed by a conceptual modern warfare approach. In a similar way, the following map was created: *The weaponized NBIC convergence map*[20] identifies the relevant innovations and tools of nano-, bio-, information technology and cognitive neuroscience within the modern warfare discussions. Applications and technologies were allocated correspondingly to the contexts they were handled within literature. A selected number of displayed applications are described in the glossary at the end. It should give an impression of how related tools from the NBIC universe work.

Most convergences are visible at the Info X Cogno intersection. A vast amount of already existing technology is gradually implemented in other contexts and thus re-contextualized. This observation is similarly the case for bio applications, differentiated by less overlapping with other disciplines. Despite a considerable relevance of nanotechnology for modern warfare, the information and neuroscience spheres are central and therefore must be understood as a reflection of what is yet to come. Many neuro applications, either invasive or non-invasive and output- or input-oriented, seek to influence the human brain. Objectives are the enhancement for advanced operability and deception, and cognitive harm. This integrates into the cognitive warfare approach that has been mentioned in the beginning of this work. Concepts in the US and China focus on the human mind to exert influence – even and particularly in a tortious manner.

Growing intersections could be expected in Bio X Cogno, taking the already important role of cognitive and neuroscience into account. Akin to the weaponization cycle, the displayed technologies and convergences might vary along their content-wise assessment by researchers and are re-locatable. These uncertainties reflect the broader picture of the NBIC convergence. As the analytical part emphasizes, with the integration of several distinct disciplines and their use in blurry or even black-box-settings, the complexity is difficult to capture comprehensively. Given the historical attention of chemi-

20 The graphical representation of the weaponized NBIC convergence map is not included as a graphic here as the high amount of technologies and innovations gathered lead to an unreadable downsizing of the systematization.

cal and bioweapons, the information age and its progress will lead to greater convergences. The Info X Cogno crossing-over will likely become stronger at the intersection with biotechnology and chemical science. It is more than imaginable that future weaponizations will spill-over into fields we might not know yet. Again, the reality of the NBIC coalescence must be assumed to be much more complex than the modelled presentation.

Cyberbiosecurity as a new resulting concept was already considered in scholarly work (here e.g., DiEuliis 2019, DeFranco 2019) and demonstrates that exploitable ground is ever growing as new domains emerge. The strong emphasis of neurotechnology, and thus cognitive (neuro-)science, arises due to neuroenhancement, neuroweapons, neurowarfare and finally neurodeterrence in the reviewed literature. In brain research, there are still huge gaps in understanding the whole functioning of the human brain. This might be an encouragement for states and non-state actors as well as terrorist groups or private companies to exploit the human brain for power advantages – given that a huge, promised gain is associated with it.

In terms of weaponization, it must be noted that not all technologies become weapons in a definitory sense as described in chapter 3.3. This process can also be partly considered as militarization of according applications – it depends on the contexts they are eventually applied in. Furthermore, inaccuracy might still pertain regarding the separation of technological applications and tools from methods. Gene drives for example serve as a method of warfare when applied with harmful intent, whereas CRISPR would be the technological innovation implemented in pathogen research and production of genetically modified organisms.

Nanotechnology was discussed and researched by scholars over the years, comparatively stable like the biotechnology arena. Despite the discussions of NBIC convergence in dual use contexts, some scholars call for a wider ranging public discussion for the benefit of transparency and trust-building. Around 15 years ago, Kosal (2009) highlighted nanotechnology as an emerging, well-funded discipline – like the biotech sphere, there is a huge potential for groundbreaking applications and unpredictable harm. Several predictions and scenarios that were built until the early 2010s within the reviewed literature have become reality. The substantial automation may serve as an example here.

Governmental initiatives and agencies have been dealing with brain mapping projects for decades. In the past 10 to 15 years the civilian sector became more relevant as a driver of innovation and applicable tech for the military. In this light, dual use research of concern (DURC) and dual use by design have evolved as concepts of critical research in technological convergence. Both approaches address the Janus-faced circumstances, whilst

DURC limits and classifies research with potentially harmful impact (Ienca et al. 2018: 269), dual use by design intends to actively supports the applicability of tech for defense purposes (Bromley and Maletta 2025: 4f.).

Generally, scenario-thinking was widespread among researchers, while most were underlining the respective threats linked to NBIC convergence as the main challenges for the 21st century. In the past couple of years though, calls for improved backing and investment became louder (i.e. in Hensing and Schlecht 2025).

These developments might sound absurdly like science fiction, but the recent acknowledgement of what once was science fiction has grown (i.e. McCreight 2024).

It seems unlikely that NBIC convergence technology would be used only or primarily defensively, as researching gene sequencing for example requires active research and could not be implemented rapidly enough when states want to react to related attacks from adversaries. For instance, brain-damaging pathogens would probably be researched under rather offensive requirements and be pursued covertly. Still, this might vary from one national capability to another. China and the US, but also Russia to some extents were central in the scholarly research of the topic. As the literature was researched in English, the strong presence of US-focused research could be explained. Regardless, the US pursued R&D in the NBIC disciplines for decades already. The Chinese counterpart started to emerge in the selected English literature since around ten years ago (i.e. Kennedy and Lim 2018, Kania 2021).

A critical observation is connected to nuclear risks and proliferation discussions, because their regulation has way more foundation than emerging threats – which do not even fall under existing conventions like the BWC or the CWC. As a result, nuclear weapons discussions turn away attention from other areas of likely conflict and weaponized tools.

While critical infrastructure must be safe and secure, uncontrolled investment in and development of neuro-, cyberbioweapons and other converging threats might appear as an expedient occasion for individual enrichment to some actors. As for now, the feasibility of some applications must be questioned and seem overestimated when conditions in the real word are not the same as in laboratories as stressed by Bruner and Lentzos (2019). Overall, the weaponization efforts are broad: even oxytocin (Tennisson and Moreno 2012) and serotonin (Crowley and Dando 2023) are targets of weaponized recontextualization.

A substantial difficulty must be considered in the use of terms. The Chinese-focused research demonstrates distinct concepts of what is being pursued and analyzed. Likewise, vague terms limit expressiveness. In the beginning of this analysis, converging and emerging disruptive were mentioned to locate NBIC technology. It demonstrates that even in the Western zone of influence, inconsistency exists to some extent. The diversity of concepts or rather adjectives, often without clear scope prevent a proper grasp in research – taking into account that heterogenous use of terms poses analytical difficulties when dealing with NBIC convergence and language limiting the expression of thoughts. In favor of successful dogmatism, an international conceptual understanding of NBIC threats and potential weapons would be desirable yet remain unrealistic under current circumstances in international relations.

Most converging tech threats target human beings, especially their cognitive and bodily functioning. Yet the exploitation and deception of nature and living organisms like insects and animals must be regarded in an economic warfare view. These living beings are likely to be exploited as vectors – carriers – of bioagents and similar risks since they are plentiful spread everywhere and reproduce quickly. Crops can be destroyed and thus destroy sources of life.

The different assessments from scholars were especially pronounced in political/strategic terms and within the awareness and scenario analysis. R&D and financial support are strongly present among leading and emerging countries, but ethical and psychological assessments were comparably less saturated. Looking into the technological aspect of applications, scholars deal with a lot of examples and their function. Yet theoretical frameworks must still be further developed – similar to the legal aspects of controlling weaponized technology and preventing the cycle from perpetuating endlessly.

While in the early 2000s a strict distinction from military use of converging technologies, including NBIC, were underlined (e.g. Nordmann 2004), recent studies emphasize the need for civil-military fusion (e.g. Bromley and Maletta 2025). The dual use by design approach became more relevant in recent years as the adaptation process from one sector to another is intended to work faster. In the same context, the classification of dual use research of concern was highlighted by scholars in the past couple of years (e.g. Ienca et al. 2018). Two distinct formations come to the surface: scholars either tend to support risk-awareness or the call for further investments and research to develop own capabilities, depending on the perspective and background of each scholar. Biberman (2021) for instance investigates the harmful effects of genetic warfare and biological weapons more strongly. McCreight (2024) similarly emphasizes potential negative outcomes and harmful applications in neuro- or computer science. Bromley and Maletta (2025) express their concerns with reference to export controls. Nevertheless, work that more centrally deals with military thought stresses the importance of own capabilities and readiness to a greater extent (e.g. Conde and Whiskeyman 2025). A seesaw might be a useful picture to explain how research is still tried to be balanced in between because scholars address the potentially unknown possibilities and threats simultaneously.

That researchers would underline the regulatory gaps related to converging weaponized NBIC technologies is probably the case due to aceleration of innovation in a short length of time, Moore's law can be mentioned in this regard. As increasingly more convergences mature, the necessity to keep sight of their use grows accordingly. Deterrence arises as a minimum goal for NBIC convergence tools, yet certain countries do not back off from covertly implementing offensive capabilities.

Similar to when chemical and biological weapons were deployed in operations, reactions from different fields, including ethicists, policy makers or legal experts, need time. A remaining issue is funding. Kosal (2009) emphasized the high amounts of research that are needed. Economically, such support should keep smaller businesses in mind. While start-ups in defense are indeed supported, national infrastructure for official governmental institutions grow.

An essential inconsistency is located in Carafano's take on the technological shift in 2005. He stated that liberal democracies would be more successful in dealing with the arising issues from new technologies. On the contrary, like Cunningham and Geis (2020) describe, China's effort in synthetic biology seek to surpass and dominate the US. At the same time, Chinese funding for R&D has begun to close the gap that exists with respect to the US, as Kania (2021) observed. Despite the primary focus on these two countries, Russia is partly highlighted as a relevant power, too (e.g. McCreight 2013).

Depending on the scholars' background, some focus on the industrial sector (e.g. DiEuliis 2019), some rather on legal issues (e.g. Bromley and Maletta 2025). Apart from that, Kosal (2009) together with Hensing and Schlecht (2025) address the non-technical barriers for innovation; the EU data privacy requirements for example exacerbate commercialization of applications in neurotech.

4.2.3 Starting points for further research

This literature review contributed to a representative overview of past and present development in this research field. Emphasized by the majority of scholars was the lack of legal embeddedness. Future frameworks should be flexible to respond to the vivid nature of NBIC technology. With the CWC and BWC there are conventions in place which should be pursued more seriously- and reliably.

In general, many of the potential unintended consequences of the mentioned and discussed applications and tools must be addressed in future research. As new fields emerge (e.g. cyberbiosecurity), researchers from various domains should step in and contribute, with understanding and clarity to new frameworks and codes of conduct as well as ethical guidelines (especially in dual use terms).

Strategic foresight, particularly in a broader sense, is lacking. Too often, approaches seem to narrow to truly grasp the complexity of the assumed future. Research must also be conducted around the societal implications in terms of trust and (de-)stabilization. The Public would undoubtedly benefit from improved debates and information on these subjects, backed by scientific evidence. In essence, the implications linked to the deployment of weaponized technologies in society and the military domain remain a wellspring for further research.

Additional starting points are located in the integration of the results into theoretical concepts and theories. They are presented in the following.

4.2.4 Theoretical integration

As the ILR intends, the results are meant to be integrated into existing theories and concepts. First and foremost, the strong focus of scholars on the cases of China and the US support the integration into the Realistic school of international relations. The China-US pair seems obvious to be integrated into the balance of power theory. It is observed that both states have strong interests in dominating the other country's position in the international system. Even though Russia is mentioned partly, the overall trend suggests a bipolar order in converging NBIC technology in a modern warfare context.

Following US-China relations that emerged from the literature, language and culture serve as another axis for theoretical integration. As prior mentioned, language is a determinant for expressions and therefore reflects the way of thinking. The existence of varying understandings of concepts like cognitive warfare could be integrated into Samuel Huntington's Clash of Civilization Theory. Here, cultural beliefs and differences become the main source of conflict. Yet, this scenario should be subject to further research, too.

With regard to the history of militarization and weaponization, life sciences probably undergo similar experiences as the biosciences did in the past. Spill-over effects come into play and the field of not only bio- but also cognitive and neuroscience become subjects of securitization.

Yet another integration of the results may be possible with the technological singularity and transhumanism. Both theories bring the human being on the one hand and technologies on the other together. Singularity in that sense entails the overall supremacy of technology, a scenario where the human species destroys itself in the end. This is certainly the most dystopian perspective for a human-machine-convergence which is driven by the analyzed enhancement efforts. Still, it highlights the harmful aspects of lack of control and regulation. Similarly, transhumanism addresses this interplay but in way less drastic ways. It aims to exploit the potential of human enhancement via technological completion, where the scenario would rather be human perfectioning. With the integration of multiple innovations, applications and devices in everyday and military life become sources of constant surveillance. In that context, the panopticon Bentham and Foucault engage with, integrates into the digital world.

4.3 Limitations of the Results

Despite this necessary contribution to the body of knowledge on weaponized NBIC technology in modern warfare, these results remain undoubtedly limited. This selection aims to be representative, thus does not include 100% of existing literature that exists on this topic. It cannot be ruled out that scientific work from other scholars addresses innovations and tools disparate from those discussed here.

Critiques must also be mentioned in terms of methodological work. The chosen framework for literature analysis could also be narrowed: types of documents included, timely interval, researched data bases, and analytical steps for data interpretation mark the adjusting screws in conducting a different kind of ILR. In this context, the steps of how each document was selected and what keywords led to the respective articles and reports could be monitored more precisely – without necessarily turning into a systematic literature review. In terms of document language, other sources could be used, e.g. when researching Chinese literature. This selection here was primarily characterized by US-focused discussions and therefore ILR in other languages of substantial states in this context would be beneficial. It is apparent that many different research approaches ensue from this spot.

Given the high velocity of research breakthroughs that is driven by political but also economic objectives, keeping pace with them needs life sciences, social sciences, and technical sciences to face unknown technological challenges of the 21st century in a multi-domain arena.

Especially the numerous links between nano, bio, info and cogno demonstrate the impossibility to reflect on disciplines separately. As the analysis here has shown, additional disciplines like chemical science are touched. Often, the biotechnology sphere is associated with chemical science and correspondingly pharmacology. Depending on the demands and interests, picking out one of the letters in NBIC would very likely produce even more reliable data and knowledge about part of these foundational technologies. This applies as much more when considering specific emerging convergences for further research – technological hubs as demonstrated in the weaponized convergence map constitute helpful starting points. Similarly, the visualizations of both the NBIC weaponization cycle and the weaponized NBIC convergence map might look different depending on other approaches of literature review. The following chapter encapsulates the ILR, its results and the future prospect.

5 Conclusion

In this analysis, around 50 documents related to the technological NBIC convergence in modern warfare were reviewed. The cognitive domain and neurotechnology were most present, which was observable at the intersection of Info X Cogno. Influencing the human brain by targeted enhancement for useful purposes and deception for malevolent purposes are among the main drivers for the intertwining of the respective NBIC disciplines. This observation aligns with the shift in modern warfare tactics, that move away from classical physical domains and target the yet unexploited mind of human species.

A central interest of this ILR was the handling of NBIC technological convergence in a modern warfare frame. This frame was built with elements from hybrid warfare, grey zone conflict, and fifth generation warfare. These elements helped to structure the reviewed literature where selected documents cover a period of around 20 years at the beginning of the 21st century. The underlying research question was:

> How do scholars assess NBIC technological convergence in terms of modern warfare at the beginning of the 21st Century?

After review, there were eight assessment types that emerged from the body of scientific research: strategic / political, financial / Resource & Development, ethical, legal, psychological, awareness-related, scenario-related, and theoretical. As chapter 4.1 showed, a strict separation of certain assessments was not feasible in a sense that overlapping was utterly present. This reflects the complexity of NBIC convergence under the auspices of modern warfare threats. More precisely, three subquestions helped to further analytically structure the assessments:

- *Where does convergence of each NBIC technology come into play?*

Literal intersections happen first and foremost where information technology and neuroscience are integrated. Neuronal systems and devices are researched, which is also true for bio-related technologies. Nano- and information technology often enable further advancements where all in all, intertwining grows. As a result, new disciplines like cyberbiosecurity evolve.

- *How are NBIC disciplines intertwined within the dual-use logic of tools?*

The scholarly work underlined that in general, almost all of the researched and applied tools and methods must be understood as dual use. It is essential to note that dual use shifts towards the understanding of useful and harmful applications in the weaponized NBIC sphere.

- *How can NBIC technology be classified from an offensive-defensive point of view?*

It was highlighted that research on neuroweapons and other enabling technologies require investment and long-term commitment. As states for instance must be prepared against attacks, e.g. on brain-computer-interfaces, defensive development plays a crucial role. But still, once a tool is developed, its deployment might be easily conducted offensively. Furthermore, weaponized technology is rather divided by overt and covert use, transforming weapon deployment into a black box.

Future research is imaginable for establishing roadmaps and scenario forecasting with focus on interdisciplinarity. Life scientists need to be more involved in these terms, for the benefit of transparency in the field and potential spill-over effects into public debates. Legal embeddedness of current developments is essential to prevent worst case scenarios from entering into reality. Ethical and psychological considerations must be included simultaneously.

This analysis has demonstrated: The future of warfare is blurry. Blurry works as core description as it touches: domains, different kinds of actors like individuals or states, multiple spheres, diverse tools – all while remaining under the threshold of declared military warfare. Ultimately, the warfare in the 21st century will be characterized by high levels of convergence, and the weapon of this future will likely be primarily covertly deployed, non-kinetic, and non-lethal.

Glossary of Selected Technologies and Tools

(f)MRI Magnetic resonance imaging is a non-implanted imaging device with high spatial revolution that measures changes in the blood flow to the brain. Sophisticated functional MRI can even record dynamic results of brain activity to map it over time, yet it is relatively costly and requires individuals to stand still during the imaging process (Hensing and Schlecht 2025).

(n)BCI Brain-Computer-Interfaces are enabler for interactions between the central nervous system and either internal or external environments. Similar to BBIs, they make direct communication to devices such as computers possible. Neuromorphic BCI adds another layer of brain exploitation by observing the brain complexity and taking the gathered information for incorporation of new knowledge but also capabilities into the brain (Sharp 2020: 317).

BBI Brain-to-Brain-Interfaces allow direct communication between brains. They are essential to potentially enable the so-called silent talk, meaning that users communicate via neural signal transmission (Mantellassi and Madziwa 2025).

Bioregulators B. consist of chemicals that can control several physiological functions in the human body, i.e. hormones (i.e. noradrenaline), cytokines (i.e. interferons), neuropeptides (i.e. NPY), neurotransmitters (i.e. dopamine) (Nixdorff et al. 2018, Lentzos 2016, Crowley and Dando 2023).

CRISPR Clustered Regularly Interspaced Short Palindromic Repeats, or ''gene scissors'', is a general class of gene editing tools and works on a specific gene sequence within the immune system of bacteria. The most commonly used variant is CRISPR/Cas 9, in which Cas 9 is the enzymatic protein that is responsible for the editing process, guided by RNA molecules. The enzyme is programmable to cut any DNA part (Cunningham and Geis 2020, Kosal 2009)

DBS	Deep brain stimulation is an invasive application to insert electrodes and implants for the modification of neural systems. For individuals with severe paralysis, they enable restoration of movement or communication. The implant happens in deep brain areas and is connected to another implant in the body, the pulse generator, to send stimulating electrical pulses (Mantellassi and Madziwa 2025, Hensing and Schlecht 2025).
DEWs	Directed energy weapons generally target the brain. Similarly to biochemical agents, their affects are on the CNS, impacting the mental and emotional states as well as mental capacity and response times. Higher cognitive functions like thought, perception, memory, and learning potentially are influenced, too (Krishnan 2016).
EEG	The Electroencephalography is a widespread and low-cost tool for recording neural activity with high temporal and low spatial resolution by applying electrodes to the skull (Hensing and Schlecht 2025).
EMF	Electromagnetic fields exert thermal and non-thermal effects on brain tissue, but also respective effects on other parts of the body, including endocrine system, visual system, cardiovascular and immune systems. As brains have a degree of electromagnetic sensitivity and responsiveness, EMF is reported to affect the CNS, brain chemistry, and histology. It also passes the BBB (McCreight 2024).
Facial Recognition T.	Facial recognition technologies refer to a type of biometric tech for recognition of individual identity by facial features. As certain military equipment entails FRTs, exports control covers them. They are intended to be dual use by design in the future; ongoing discussion exist on adding further categories of export control (Bromley and Maletta 2025).
Gene Drive	Gene drives are tools to dispense a genetic modification through entire populations. They spread generationally which makes them less due to target humans. A weaponized application could mean to use rapidly reproducing species (insects, bacteria) into ecosystems in order for them to collapse by potentially eliminating entire species. Still, their

effects are limited to a single trait and are rather relevant for economic warfare (Cunningham and Geis 2020).

MNE Machine neurobehavioral engineering refers to a COGINT tactic in which advanced data analytics as well as psychometric profiling are integrated aiming to pursue precise and individualized cognitive influence operations. It rather less targets broad populations and thus fuses different data streams to construct detailed cognitive profiles: from social media activity, to behavioral patterns to biometric data (Conde and Whiskeyman 2025).

Modafinil Modafinil is a narcolepsy treatment drug discovered in the 1970s. It has shown to improve working memory and enhance the executive functioning in non-sleep-deprived individuals. It might have been used in Iraq by the French Army in the 1990s and US Air Force in 2003 as it strengthens alertness and concentration which was important during long flights (Lentzos 2016).

Neural Lace Neural lace are threads of miniature electrodes. They are connected through biocompatible polymer and need syringe injection to be transferred into the brain non-surgically. A mesh roll thus expands and then distributes microelectrodes to mimic the brain tissue flexibility. This tool can connect neural pathways and monitor injury sites, to date only in mice. The lace is minimally damaging and extreme thin (Hensing and Schlecht 2025).

Neural Networks Neural Networks are core elements of Deep Learning and AI as they provide the basis for applications such as voice and facial recognition or language to text adaptation to model the human brain's learning aptitude (Rashid 2024).

NIS Neuronal interface systems are a group of invasive and non-invasive brain applications aiming to restore brain functioning or improve it. Examples are inter alia EEG, (f)MRI, retinal vision implants, DBS, and nearinfrared spectroscopy (MacKellar 2019).

Optogenetics O. are photoactive proteins meaning that they are stimulated with high precision by using light. They are injected into the brain and genetically modify neurons. Via optical fibre integration the recording of neural activity might be used for sensing (Hensing and Schlecht 2025).

Propranolol P. is a beta-blocker and cognitive enhancement drug, deployed to suppress the formation of painful memories in veterans (Krishnan 2016).

RAM Restoring Active Memory is a neural interface seeking to either facilitate memory formation or retrieve existing memory (MacKellar 2019).

Scalar waves S. waves are three-dimensional self-contained waves, spinning on one fixes axis. The belong to the non-linear waves group and operate at frequencies aligned with Schumann resonances (part of the Earth's electromagnetic field spectrum) and arise from electrical activity between Earth surface and ionosphere. The electromagnetic waves are light-generated and are supposed to have effects on humans, i.e. influencing cellular, neuronic and immune suppressing factors (Krishnan 2016).

tDCS Transcranial Direct current stimulation are portable devices with adaptation possibilities to different settings, using low electrical flow for brain modulation (Gielas 2025).

Toxins T. are noxious chemicals that were obtained from living organisms; i.e. Anatoxin A, botulinum toxin, saxitoxin. (Nixdorff et al. 2018)

Ultra-Wide Band R. S. Ultra-wide band radar systems make it possible for soldiers to get a presentation of 3D images of people and objects that would otherwise be hidden behind barriers. The small sensors are portable and allow insight from multiple angles. They were developed by Israeli stakeholder for operations in Jenin and other Palestinian cities (Halper 2015).

References

Altmann, Jürgen (2020): New Military Technologies: Dangers for International Security and Peace. In *S+F* 38 (1), pp. 36–42. DOI: 10.5771/0175-274X-2020-1-36.

Baker, James E. (2021): Arms Control by Analogy. In *The Centaur's Dilemma: National Security Law for the Coming AI Revolution.* Brookings Institution Press, pp. 178–224. Available online at http://www.jstor.org/stable/10.7864/j.ctvktrx1w.11.

Balakrishnan, Bhaskar (2011): Role of Technology in India's Foreign Relations. In *Indian Foreign Affairs Journal* 6 (1), pp. 70–86. Available online at http://www.jstor.org/stable/45340872.

Biberman, Yelena (2021): The Technologies and International Politics of Genetic Warfare. In *Strategic Studies Quarterly* 15 (3), pp. 6–33. Available online at https://www.jstor.org/stable/48618294.

Bosch, Olivia; van Ham, Peter (2007): UNSCR 1540: Its Future and Contribution to Global Non-Proliferation and Counter-Terrorism. In Olivia Bosch, Peter van Ham (Eds.): *Global Non-Proliferation and Counter-Terrorism.* Brookings Institution Press, pp. 207–226. Available online at http://www.jstor.org/stable/10.7864/j.ctt127zz0.18.

Bredow, Wilfried von (2024): Kriege im 21. Jahrhundert. Wie heute militärische Konflikte geführt werden. BeBra Verlag.

Bromley, Mark; Maletta, Giovanna (2025): *The Militarization of Technology: Preventing Diversion and Misuse Through Export Controls*. Stockholm International Peace Research Institute.

Bruner, Robert C.; Lentzos, Filippa (2019): Militarising the Mind: Assessing the Weapons of the Ultimate Battlefield. In *BioSocieties* 14 (1), pp. 94–122. DOI: 10.1057/s41292-018-0121-4.

Bundesamt für Bevölkerungsschutz und Katastrophenhilfe (2025): *CBRN Schutz*. Available online at https://www.bbk.bund.de/DE/Themen/CBRN-Schutz/cbrn-schutz_node.html, checked on 23 February 2026.

Caduff, Carlo (2008): Anticipations of Biosecurity. In Andrew Lakoff, Stephen J. Collier (Eds.): *Biosecurity Interventions*. Columbia University Press, pp. 257–278. Available online at http://www.jstor.org/stable/10.7312/lako14606.12.

Carafano, James Jay (2005): Sustaining Military Capabilities in the 21st Century: Rethinking the Utility of the Principles of War. In *American Intelligence Journal* 23, pp. 67–72. Available online at http://www.jstor.org/stable/44327040.

Citino, Robert (2012): *Technology in the Persian Gulf War of 1991*. History Now. Available online at https://www.gilderlehrman.org/history-resources/essays/technology-persian-gulf-war-1991, checked on 1 February 2026.

Clapp, Sebastian (2022): *At a Glance. Emerging disruptive technologies in defence*. European Parliament. EPRS – European Parliamentary Research Service. Available online at https://www.europarl.europa.eu/RegData/etudes/ATAG/2022/733647/EPRS_ATA(2022)733647_EN.pdf, checked on 23 February 2026.

Claverie, Bernard; Cluzel, François (2022): *"Cognitive Warfare": The Advent of the Concept of "Cognitics" in the Field of Warfare*. First NATO Scientific Meeting on Cognitive Warfare (France), 21 June 2021. Available online at https://hal.science/hal-03635889/document, checked on 23 February 2026.

Concini, Alessandro de; Toth, Jaroslav (2019): *The space sector and its business models*. European Investment Bank. Available online at http://www.jstor.org/stable/resrep52266.6, checked on 23 February 2025.

Conde, Jorge; Whiskeyman, Andrew (2025): The Emergence of Cognitive Intelligence (COGINT) as a New Military Intelligence Collection Discipline. In *International Journal of Intelligence and Counterintelligence* (online first), pp. 1–27. DOI: 10.1080/08850607.2025.2571497.

Crowley, Michael; Dando, Malcolm (2023): Lost in the Gap. Toxin and Bioregulator Weapons. In *Arms Control Today* 53 (3), pp. 11–17. Available online at https://www.jstor.org/stable/27227698.

Cunningham, Marcus A.; Geis, John P. (2020): A National Strategy for Synthetic Biology. In *Strategic Studies Quarterly* 14 (3), pp. 49–80. Available online at https://www.jstor.org/stable/26937411.

DeFranco, Joseph; DiEuliis, Diane; Giordano, James (2019): Redefining Neuroweapons. Emerging Capabilities in Neuroscience and Neurotechnology. In *PRISM* 8 (3), pp. 48–63. Available online at https://www.jstor.org/stable/26864276.

DiEuliis, Diane (2019): Key National Security Questions for the Future of Synthetic Biology. In *The Fletcher Forum of World Affairs* 43 (1), pp. 127–143. Available online at http://www.jstor.org/stable/45289832.

Eads, L. J.; Clarke, Ryan; Lin, Xiaoxu Sean; McCreight, Robert (2023): *Warfare in the Cognitive Age: NeuroStrike and the PLA's Advanced Psychological Weapons & Tactics*. CCP Biothreats Initiative, Available online at https://static1.squarespace.com/static/6444894f2a886e74091c9e1b/t/65824d9fd6d294583d8e859c/1703038367948/Warfare+in+the+Cognitive+Age+NeuroStrike+and+the+PLAs+Advanced+Psychological+Weapons+%26+Tactics.pdf, checked on 20 December 2025.

European Commission (2025): *European strategy on research and technology infrastructures* [Press release]. Available online at https://ec.europa.eu/commission/presscorner/api/files/document/print/en/ip_25_2097/IP_25_2097_EN.pdf, checked on 20 December 2025.

European Commission – European Political Strategy Centre (2025): *The future of European competitiveness. Part A: A competitiveness strategy for Europe*. Publications Office of the European Union. Available online at https://commission.europa.eu/document/download/97e481fd-2dc3-412d-be4c-f152a8232961_en?filename=The%20future%20of%20European%20competitiveness%20_%20A%20competitiveness%20strategy%20for%20Europe.pdf, checked on 20 December 2025.

Evron, Yoram (2025): Israel's defence industry: adaptation and growth in a changing arms market. In *Defence Studies* 25 (2), pp. 301–321. DOI: 10.1080/14702436.2025.2472720.

Federal Bureau of Investigation (2016): *Amerithrax or Anthrax Investigation*. Available online at https://www.fbi.gov/history/famous-cases/amerithrax-or-anthrax-investigation, checked on 23 February 2026.

Frieß, Johannes L.; Giese, Bernd; Rößing, Anna; Jeremias, Gunnar (2020): Towards a prospective assessment of the power and impact of Novel Invasive Environmental Biotechnologies. In *S+F* 38 (1), pp. 29–35. DOI: 10.5771/0175-274X-2020-1-29.

Frinking, Erik; Sweijs, Tim; van Dongen, Teun; Ethembabaoglu, Aksel (2009): *Navigating the CBRN landscape of 2010 and beyond: towards a new policy paradigm*. Hague Centre for Strategic Studies. Available online at http://www.jstor.org/stable/resrep12592.8, checked on 23 February 2026.

Gielas, Anna M. (2025): Fast and flawed: how emerging neurotechnologies can speed up and break down military decision-making processes. In *Defense & Security Analysis* 42 (1), pp. 1–24. DOI: 10.1080/14751798.2025.2524284.

Goodman, Marc; Khanna, Parag (2013): The Power of Moore's Law in a World of Geotechnology. In *The National Interest* 123, pp. 64–73. Available online at http://www.jstor.org/stable/42896538.

Gut, Ulrich (2025): *Si vis pacem, para bellum!*. PolitReflex. Available online at https://politreflex.ch/si-vis-pacem-para-bellum/, checked on 1 February 2026.

Halper, Jeff (2015): Dominant Maneuver. In *War Against the People: Israel, the Palestinians and Global Pacification*. Pluto Press, pp. 97–112. Available online at http://www.jstor.org/stable/j.ctt183pct7.10.

Hayes, Peter; Cavazos, Roger (2015): Complexity and Weapons of Mass Destruction in Northeast Asia. In Peter Hayes, Kiho Yi (Eds.): *Complexity, Security and Civil Society in East Asia*. Cambridge, Open Book Publishers, pp. 263–320.

Hensing, Jakob; Schlecht, Peter (2025): *Neurotechnology, Brain-Computer Interfaces, and Implications for Germany's and Europe's Foreign & Security Policy*. Global Public Policy Institute. Available online at https://gppi.net/assets/HensingSchlecht_ActionPotentials_2025_Web.pdf, checked on 10 December 2025.

Hill, Mike (2022): *On posthuman war. Computation and military violence*. University of Minnesota Press.

Ienca, Marcello; Jotterand, Fabrice; Elger, Bernice S. (2018): From Healthcare to Warfare and Reverse: How Should We Regulate Dual-Use Neurotechnology? In *Neuron* 97 (2), pp. 269–274. DOI: 10.1016/j.neuron.2017.12.017.

Kania, Elsa B. (2019): Minds at War. China's Pursuit of Military Advantage through Cognitive Science and Biotechnology. In *PRISM* 8 (3), pp. 82–101. Available online at https://www.jstor.org/stable/26864278.

Kania, Elsa B. (2021): China's Drive for Innovation within a World of Profound Changes. In *Asia Policy* 16 (2), pp. 17–32. Available online at https://www.jstor.org/stable/27023968.

Kennedy, Andrew B.; Lim, Darren J. (2018): The innovation imperative. Technology and US–China rivalry in the twenty-first century. In *International Affairs* 94 (3), pp. 553–572. Available online at https://www.jstor.org/stable/48767845.

Koblentz, Gregory D. (2012): From biodefence to biosecurity: The Obama administration's strategy for countering biological threats. In *International Affairs* 88 (1), pp. 131–148. Available online at http://www.jstor.org/stable/41428545.

Kosal, Margaret (2009): Nanotechnology for Chemical and Biological Defense. Springer New York.

Kosal, Margaret; Putney, Joy (2023): Neurotechnology and international security: Predicting commercial and military adoption of brain-computer interfaces (BCIs) in the United States and China. In *Politics and the Life Sciences: The Journal of the Association for Politics and the Life Sciences* 42 (1), pp. 81–103. DOI: 10.1017/pls.2022.2.

Kosal, Margaret E. (2020): Emerging Life Sciences and Possible Threats to International Security. In *Orbis* 64 (4), pp. 599–614. DOI: 10.1016/j.orbis.2020.08.008.

Kosal, Margaret E.; Huang, Jonathan Y. (2015): Security implications and governance of cognitive neuroscience. In *Politics and the Life Sciences: The Journal of the Association for Politics and the Life Sciences* 34 (1), pp. 93–108. DOI: 10.1017/pls.2015.4.

Krishnan, Armin (2016): Attack on the Brain: Neurowars and Neurowarfare. In *Space and Defense* 9 (1), Article 4. DOI: 10.32873/uno.dc.sd.09.01.1110.

Krishnan, Armin (2022): Fifth Generation Warfare, Hybrid Warfare, and Gray Zone Conflict: A Comparison. In *Journal of Strategic Security* 15 (4), pp. 14–31. DOI: 10.5038/1944-0472.15.4.2013.

Lentzos, Filippa (2016): Biology's Misuse Potential. In *Connections QJ* 15 (2), pp. 48–64. DOI: 10.11610/Connections.15.2.04.

MacKellar, Calum (2019): Neuronal Interface Systems. In Calum MacKellar (Ed.): *Cyborg Mind: What Brain–Computer and Mind–Cyberspace Interfaces Mean for Cyberneuroethics*. Berghahn Books, pp. 43–98. Available online at http://www.jstor.org/stable/j.ctvvb7mw5.8.

Mantellassi, Federico; Madziwa, Edward (2025): *Neurotechnology in the Military Domain: A Primer*. United Nations Institute for Disarmament Research (UNIDIR). Available online at https://unidir.org/wp-content/uploads/2025/11/UNIDIR_Neurotechnology_Military-Domain_A-Primer.pdf.

Marjanović, Arijana; Smiljanić, Dražen (2025): *Cognitive Warfare – The Human Mind as the New Battlefield.* Proceedings of the Defence and Security Conference 2025 (Zagreb), pp. 84–114.

Mayer, Michael (2023): *Multi-Domain Operations, Emerging Military Technology and the Future of Manoeuvre Warfare*. Norwegian Defence Research Establishment; NATO Science and Technology Organization. Available online at https://publications.sto.nato.int/publications/STO%20Meeting%20Proceedings/STO-MP-SAS-OCS-ORA-2023/MP-SAS-OCS-ORA-2023-08.pdf.

Mazarr, Michael J.; Kerrigan, Amanda; Lenain, Benjamin (2025): *Stabilizing the U.S.-China Rivalry*. RAND Corporation.

McCreight, Robert (2013): Convergent Technologies and Future Strategic Security Threats. In *Strategic Studies Quarterly* 7 (4), pp. 11–19. Available online at http://www.jstor.org/stable/26270775.

McCreight, Robert (2024): The war inside your mind: unprotected brain battlefields and neuro-vulnerability. In *Academia Biology* 2 (1), pp. 1–9. DOI: 10.20935/AcadBiol6156.

Meier, Ernst-Christoph; Kamp, Karl-Heinz; zum Meyer Felde, Rainer (2021): *Wörterbuch zur Sicherheitspolitik. Deutschland in einem veränderten internationalen Umfeld*, 9. Auflage. Mittler.

Minvielle, Nicolas; Roussie, Marie; Thomas, Romane (2025): *Future of Conflicts. A Vision of What Is to Come*. NATO Defense College. Available online at https://www.ndc.nato.int/download/what-foresight-does-nato-need/?wpdmdl=10067&refresh=6909cf5c78a261762250588, checked on 1 January 2026.

Montocchio, Philippe (2021): La guerre cognitique. Avant propos – par le directeur adjoint du Collaboration Support Office de l'Organisation pour la Science et la Technologie (STO) de l'OTAN. In Claverie Bernard, Prébot Baptiste, Cluzel Du François (Eds.): *Cognitive Warfare, La guerre cognitique.* NATO Collaboration Support Office, pp. VII–VIII. Available online at https://hal.science/hal-03425401.

NATO Review (2021): *Countering cognitive warfare: awareness and resilience.* Johns Hopkins University, Imperial College London. Available online at https://www.nato.int/docu/review/articles/2021/05/20/countering-cognitive-warfare-awareness-and-resilience/index.html, checked on 11 November 2025.

Nixdorff, Kathryn; Borisova, Tatiana; Komisarenko, Serhiy; Dando, Malcolm (2018): Dual-use nano-neurotechnology. In *Politics and the Life Sciences* 37 (2), pp. 180–202. DOI: 10.1017/pls.2018.15.

Nordmann, Alfred (2004): *Converging Technologies – Shaping the Future of European Societies.* High Level Expert Group "Foresighting the New Technology Wave". Available online at https://pure.iiasa.ac.at/id/eprint/12590/1/Converging%20Technologies.pdf, checked on 23 February 2026.

Oermann, Marilyn H.; Hays, Judith C. (2016): *Writing for publication in nursing.* 3rd edition. Springer New York.

Ortmann, Matyas (2024): *Another potential aspect of the military revolution: Nanotechnology as a key element of NATO's future.* Defense and Security Magazine. Available online at https://www.defensemagazine.com/article/another-potential-aspect-of-the-military-revolution-nanotechnology-as-a-key-element-of-natos-future.

Prust, Oscar (2025): *Parlamentarische Rüstungskontrolle. Neue Technologien und Sicherheitspolitik in der Kontroverse.* Dissertation, Schriftenreihe des Wissenschaftlichen Forums für Internationale Sicherheit e.V., Band 37. Barbara Budrich Verlag.

Rashid, Tariq (2024): Neuronale Netze selbst programmieren. Ein verständlicher Einstieg mit Python. 2. Auflage. O'Reilly.

Raska, Michael (2019): Strategic Competition for Emerging Military Technologies. Comparative Paths and Patterns. In *PRISM* 8 (3), pp. 64–81. Available online at https://www.jstor.org/stable/26864277.

Roco, Mihail C.; Bainbridge, William Sims (2002): Converging Technologies for Improving Human Performance. Nanotechnology, Biotechnology, Information Technology and Cognitive Science. Springer.

Rosenbach, Eric et al. (2025): *Critical and Emerging Technologies Index*, Belfer Center for Science and International Affairs.

Rychnovská, Dagmar (2016): Governing dual-use knowledge: From the politics of responsible science to the ethicalization of security. In *Security Dialogue* 47 (4), pp. 310–328. DOI: 10.1177/0967010616658848.

Schimroszik, Nadine (2025): *Ferngesteuerte Kakerlaken als Bio-Roboter.* Handelsblatt. Available online at https://www.handelsblatt.com/unternehmen/start-ups/ruestung-ferngesteuerte-kakerlaken-als-bio-roboter/100136268.html, checked on 23 February 2026.

Senarak, Chalermpong (2024): Port cyberattacks from 2011 to 2023: a literature review and discussion of selected cases. In *Maritime Economics & Logistics* 26 (1), pp. 105–130. DOI: 10.1057/s41278-023-00276-8.

Shanahan, Murray (2015): *The technological singularity*. Cambridge/London.

Sharp, Carolyn (2020): Cognitively Enhanced Humans as Both Warfighters and Weapons of War. In *University of Florida Journal of Law & Public Policy* 32 (2), Article 4. Available online at https://scholarship.law.ufl.edu/jlpp/vol32/iss2/4/.

Steininger, Rolf (2020): *Der Vietnamkrieg*. Bundeszentrale für Politische Bildung. Available online at https://www.bpb.de/themen/nordamerika/usa/317398/der-vietnamkrieg/, checked on 2 January 2026.

Swedish Defence University (2025): *DNA as a power tool in hybrid warfare*. Available online at https://www.fhs.se/en/swedish-defence-university/stories/2025-03-31-dna-as-a-power-tool-in-hybrid-warfare.html, checked on 2 January 2026.

Tennison, Michael N.; Moreno, Jonathan D. (2012): Neuroscience, ethics, and national security: the state of the art. In *PLOS Biology* 10 (3), e1001289. DOI: 10.1371/journal.pbio.1001289.

Torraco, Richard J. (2005): Writing Integrative Literature Reviews: Guidelines and Examples. In *Human Resource Development Review* 4 (3), pp. 356–367. DOI: 10.1177/1534484305278283.

Torraco, Richard J. (2016): Writing Integrative Literature Reviews: Using the Past and Present to Explore the Future. In *Human Resource Development Review* 15 (4), pp. 404–428. DOI: 10.1177/1534484316671606.

Subject Index

The Author

Alisa Grunert completed her Bachelor and Master in Political Science and Sociology at the Martin Luther University Halle-Wittenberg – including a short-term study program at the Centre International de Formation Européenne. Her research interest lies in the intersection between security studies and cognitive science, particularly with regard to the weaponization of converging technologies in future warfare.